RISKPRO's

THE KYC GUIDE

A Comprehensive Handbook for
Certified KYC Experts

© **CA Mayur Joshi**
Apurva Joshi
Certified Anti Money Laundering Expert

INTRODUCTION

© RISKPRO

ISBN 978-1-312-44201-6

Price: $50

Printed in India

Published by:

Riskpro Publication

Riskpro Management Consulting Pvt Ltd

209,Indulal Commercial Complex, L.B.Shastri Road,Navi Peth,

Pune-411030 India

Visit us at www.riskprolearning.com

Printing and Publishing rights reserved with Riskpro Management Consulting Pvt.Ltd. No part of this book may be reproduced in any manner whatsoever or translated in any other language without permission in writing from Riskpro Management Consulting Pvt Ltd.

Authors and publishers have made all the efforts to avoid errors and omissions in this publication. In spite of this, errors may creep in. Any Mistake, Error or discrepancy noted may be brought to our notice which shall be taken care of in the next edition. It is notified that neither publisher, nor the author or seller will be responsible for any damage or loss of action to anyone, of any kind, in any manner there from. and are not responsible for the consequences, whatsoever, of any action taken on the basis of this book.

The book is authored by CA Mayur Joshi and Apurva Joshi– Certified Anti Money Laundering Expert. For any questions relating to the books author can be reached at contactus@riskpro.co.in

TABLE OF CONTENTS

Introduction 10
    Importance of KYC 11
        Compliance with regulatory requirements 11
        Prevention of fraud and financial crimes 11
        Enhanced due diligence for high-risk customers 11
        Protecting the reputation of financial institutions 12
        Ensuring compliance with international standards 12
        Facilitating financial inclusion 12
    Understanding KYC in India 13
        Definition of KYC 13
        Brief history of KYC regulations in India 13
        Benefits of KYC in India 15
        Role of banks and FI's in KYC 16
        Limitations in Implementing KYC in India 17
    PML Amendments in 2023 18
        Group-wide Policies 18
        Non-profit Organizations (NPOs) 19
        Politically Exposed Persons (PEPs) 20
        Beneficial Ownership 20
        Additional Documentation 21
        Virtual Digital Assets (VDAs) 21
        Record Keeping and Reporting 22
        The Inclusion of Practicing Professionals 23

KYC Methods Prevalent in India 25
    Types of KYC Processes 25
        Paper-Based KYC 26
        Aadhaar-based KYC 28
        Digital KYC 35
        Offline KYC 36

INTRODUCTION

    Central KYC 40

    Video KYC 45

Identification documents required for KYC 53

Address proof documents required for KYC 54

KYC for Different Industries 57

KYC in Banking and Financial Services 58

    Personal Information 59

    Identification Documents 59

    Proof of Address 59

    Financial Records 59

    Politically Exposed Persons (PEPs) 59

    Sanction Lists and Adverse Media Screening 60

    Ongoing Monitoring 60

KYC in Telecom 60

    Identity Fraud 61

    eKYC in Telecom 61

    Biometric Verification 63

    Regulatory Framework 65

KYC in Insurance 66

    KYC processes accepted by IRDAI 67

    KYC for Individual Customers 69

    KYC for Juridical Persons 70

KYC in E-commerce 71

    Steps in KYC Process of eCommerce 73

    Case Studies on eCommerce KYC 74

KYC in Gaming 75

    Challenges of ID Verification for Casinos 78

KYC in Real Estate 79

    Regulations Governing Real Estate 80

    Examples of KYC Requirements in Real Estate 81

KYC On-boarding Program 84

- Customer Identification 84
- Customer Due Diligence (CDD) 86
  - Source of Funds/Wealth 88
  - Politically Exposed Persons (PEP) Screening 90
  - Sanctions and Watchlist Screening 91
  - Adverse Media Checks 93
  - Risk Scoring 95
- Ongoing Monitoring 98

KYC Compliance and Regulatory Framework 101
- Prevention of Money Laundering Act (PMLA) 102
  - Enhanced Due Diligence 104
  - Ongoing Due Diligence and Transaction Monitoring 105
- Role of RBI in KYC compliance 107
  - Customer Acceptance Policy (CAP) 108
- Risk Management 110
- Customer Identification 111
- Customer Due Diligence 112
  - CDD For Sole Proprietors 115
  - CDD for Legal Entities 116
- Ultimate Beneficial Owner 117
  - UBOs in Company 118
  - UBOs in Firms 118
  - UBOs of AOP/BOI 118
  - Exception of UBO Identification 119
- On Going Due Diligence 119
  - Updating KYC 120
- KYC Audits and Inspections 123

Challenges in KYC Compliance 128
- Challenges faced by regulated entities 130
- Challenges faced by customers 130
- Challenges faced by the government 131

INTRODUCTION

Addressing the challenges 132
KYC and Digital Transformation **134**
    ROLE OF TECHNOLOGY IN KYC 135
        Online Forms and Document Submission 135
        Data Analytics and Artificial Intelligence (AI) 137
        Electronic Data Sources 138
        Workflow Automation 146
    Advantages of Digital KYC 149
    Risks and Challenges in KYC 150
        False Positives 151
        Poor Data Quality 152
        Lack of Detailed Alerts 152
        Inadequate Record Keeping 153
        Limited Configurability 155
        Holistic Approach to Compliance 156
        Amber Management Monitoring 157
Role of FIU **160**
    Registration with FIU-IND 162
    Appointment of AML Officers 163
        Principal Officer (PO) 163
        Designated Director 165
    Reports to be Submitted to FIU 167
Future of KYC in India **169**
    Emerging Trends in KYC 169
        Digitization and Automation 169
        Risk-based Approach 171
        Use of Artificial Intelligence (AI) and Machine Learning (ML) 173
        Biometric Authentication 174
    Potential Impact of Emerging Technologies on KYC 177
    Future of KYC Regulations in India 178
        Unified KYC 178

INTRODUCTION

    Digital Transformation 180

    Enhanced Data Security 180

Practice Questions **182**

References **190**

WHAT IS CKYCE?

The Certified KYC Expert (CKYCE) program offered by Indiaforensic is a comprehensive certification program that focuses on enhancing the capabilities of KYC teams.

The program equips professionals with the necessary knowledge and skills to effectively handle KYC verification processes within organizations.

CKYCE professionals are trained in various aspects of KYC, including understanding regulatory requirements, conducting thorough customer due diligence, and implementing effective risk management practices.

By gaining expertise in these areas, CKYCE professionals play a crucial role in ensuring compliance with KYC regulations and mitigating the risks associated with money laundering and financial fraud.

This certification program is particularly beneficial for entry-level professionals who are looking to establish a career in the AML domain. It provides them with a solid foundation of knowledge and practical skills required to excel in KYC-related roles. By obtaining the CKYCE certification, these professionals demonstrate their commitment to maintaining the highest standards of compliance and contribute to the overall integrity of the financial services industry.

INTRODUCTION

With the rapid evolution of technology and the increasing prevalence of financial crimes, organizations are recognizing the importance of having qualified KYC experts on their teams. The CKYCE program offered by Indiaforensic addresses this need by equipping professionals with the necessary expertise to handle the complexities of customer KYC verification. By enrolling in this program, individuals can enhance their career prospects and make valuable contributions to the organizations they serve.

The Certified KYC Expert program is designed to empower professionals with the knowledge, skills, and certification needed to excel in the field of KYC compliance. It serves as a stepping stone for entry-level professionals to establish themselves in the AML domain and make a positive impact in combating financial crimes.

CKYCE certification course is however different from the Certified Anti Money Laundering Expert (CAME) program offered by Indiaforensic.

While both certifications are valuable in their respective domains, the CKYCE program caters to professionals who primarily focus on customer KYC verification, while the CAME program targets professionals engaged in comprehensive anti-money laundering activities. The CAME program offers a broader scope by encompassing the entire field of anti-money laundering.

INTRODUCTION

It is designed for experienced financial crime professionals who are involved in transaction monitoring, AML compliance, and AML investigations. The CAME program delves into advanced topics such as money laundering techniques, regulatory frameworks, risk assessments, suspicious activity reporting, and international cooperation.

INTRODUCTION

KYC, which stands for "Know Your Customer," is a process of verifying the identity of customers as a precautionary measure to prevent illegal activities such as money laundering and terrorist financing. In India, KYC is mandatory for individuals and businesses who want to open a bank account, obtain a credit card, or invest in financial products such as mutual funds, insurance policies, and stocks.

The Indian government and regulatory bodies such as the Reserve Bank of India (RBI) and the Securities and Exchange Board of India (SEBI) have implemented various guidelines and regulations to ensure the smooth and efficient implementation of KYC procedures. The KYC process involves the collection and verification of personal information and documents such as proof of identity, address, and income.

KYC is an important process as it helps to establish the identity of customers, mitigate the risk of fraud, and promote financial inclusion. In this course, we will dive deeper into the various aspects of KYC in India and explore its impact on the financial system, businesses, and individuals.

IMPORTANCE OF KYC

KYC plays a crucial role in maintaining the integrity of the financial system in India. It helps to prevent money laundering, terrorist financing, and other financial crimes by ensuring that the identities of customers are verified and authenticated. The importance of KYC can be understood in the following ways:

COMPLIANCE WITH REGULATORY REQUIREMENTS

KYC is a regulatory requirement that financial institutions must comply with in India. The Reserve Bank of India (RBI) has mandated the implementation of KYC guidelines to prevent financial fraud and money laundering. Failure to comply with KYC guidelines can result in significant fines and penalties.

PREVENTION OF FRAUD AND FINANCIAL CRIMES

KYC helps to prevent financial fraud and other financial crimes by ensuring that the identities of customers are verified and authenticated. It reduces the risk of identity theft and other fraudulent activities, such as opening bank accounts with fake identities.

ENHANCED DUE DILIGENCE FOR HIGH-RISK CUSTOMERS

KYC requires enhanced due diligence for high-risk customers, such as politically exposed persons (PEPs) and high net worth individuals (HNIs). This ensures that financial institutions are aware of the risks associated with these customers and take appropriate measures to prevent financial crimes.

INTRODUCTION

PROTECTING THE REPUTATION OF FINANCIAL INSTITUTIONS

KYC helps financial institutions to protect their reputation by ensuring that they do not engage in activities that are associated with financial crimes. It helps to establish a relationship of trust between financial institutions and their customers.

ENSURING COMPLIANCE WITH INTERNATIONAL STANDARDS

KYC is also important for ensuring compliance with international standards, such as the Financial Action Task Force (FATF)[i] recommendations. India is a member of the FATF, and compliance with KYC guidelines is essential for maintaining India's position as a responsible member of the international financial community.

FACILITATING FINANCIAL INCLUSION

KYC also plays an essential role in facilitating financial inclusion. By verifying the identities of customers, financial institutions can open accounts for previously unbanked individuals, thereby providing them with access to financial services. This promotes financial inclusion and economic development.

KYC[ii] is a critical component of the Indian financial system. It helps to prevent financial fraud and money laundering, protects the reputation of financial institutions, ensures compliance with regulatory requirements and international standards, and facilitates financial inclusion. Financial institutions must comply with KYC guidelines to maintain the integrity of the financial system and prevent financial crimes.

UNDERSTANDING KYC IN INDIA

DEFINITION OF KYC

KYC stands for "Know Your Customer" or "Know Your Client". It is a process of identifying and verifying the identity of customers or clients by businesses, especially financial institutions, to ensure that they are not involved in any illegal or fraudulent activities. The KYC process involves collecting and verifying personal information of the customer, such as their name, address, date of birth, occupation, and other relevant details. KYC is an important regulatory requirement in many countries to prevent money laundering, terrorism financing, and other financial crimes. in India, KYC is a mandatory requirement for opening bank accounts, investing in securities or mutual funds, and availing other financial services. The Reserve Bank of India (RBI) has mandated the KYC process for all financial institutions operating in the country. The main objective of KYC in India is to prevent money laundering, terrorist financing, and other financial crimes by ensuring that financial institutions have complete information about their customers or clients.

BRIEF HISTORY OF KYC REGULATIONS IN INDIA

The Indian government has taken several steps to regulate the financial sector and curb the menace of money laundering and terrorist financing. The Reserve Bank of India (RBI), India's central bank, first introduced KYC guidelines in 2002, which required banks to undertake certain customer identification procedures while opening accounts for their customers. However, these guidelines were not mandatory, and compliance was left to the discretion of individual banks.

INTRODUCTION

In 2004, the Prevention of Money Laundering Act (PMLA) was enacted, which laid down the legal framework for combating money laundering in India. The act mandated financial institutions to undertake KYC procedures for all their customers and maintain records of their transactions.

In 2005, the RBI made KYC compliance mandatory for all banks, financial institutions, and intermediaries dealing in securities. This meant that every bank or financial institution was required to carry out customer due diligence (CDD) measures, including identification and verification of their customers' identity, residential address, and other relevant details.

In 2012, the Indian government issued guidelines for KYC compliance for all types of financial institutions, including banks, insurance companies, and mutual funds. The guidelines were based on the recommendations of the Financial Action Task Force (FATF), an inter-governmental body that sets international standards for combating money laundering and terrorist financing.

In 2016, the Indian government introduced the Aadhaar-based e-KYC system, which allowed customers to provide their Aadhaar card as a valid proof of identity and address while opening a bank account. The system made the KYC process faster and more efficient and also helped in reducing the cost of compliance for banks and other financial institutions.

In 2021, the RBI issued new guidelines for KYC compliance, which included the use of video-based KYC for customer identification and verification, in addition to the existing methods of physical document verification and Aadhaar-based e-KYC.

The history of KYC regulations in India shows that the government has been proactive in implementing measures to combat money laundering and terrorist financing. The introduction of Aadhaar-based e-KYC and video-based KYC has made the process of customer due diligence faster and more efficient, while also ensuring compliance with the regulatory requirements.

BENEFITS OF KYC IN INDIA

KYC contributes to a safer and more secure financial ecosystem, reducing the risks associated with financial crimes, enhancing customer protection, and fostering trust between financial institutions and customers. It also helps in achieving regulatory compliance and promoting inclusive growth by extending financial services to previously unbanked or underbanked segments of the population. KYC has several benefits for the Indian financial system and economy, including:

1. Preventing financial crimes: KYC norms help prevent money laundering, terrorist financing, and other financial crimes by verifying customer identity and maintaining transaction records.
2. Enhancing financial inclusion: KYC norms help banks and financial institutions verify customer identity and address, making it easier for individuals and businesses to access financial services.
3. Strengthening customer trust: KYC norms help build customer trust by ensuring that financial institutions

take adequate measures to protect customer information and prevent identity theft.
4. Facilitating cross-border transactions: KYC norms help facilitate cross-border transactions by providing a standard framework for verifying customer identity and complying with international regulations.

ROLE OF BANKS AND FI'S IN KYC

Banks play a critical role in KYC (Know Your Customer) procedures as they are required by law to implement them to mitigate the risk of money laundering, terrorist financing, and other financial crimes. Banks need to verify the identity of their customers and collect relevant information about them, such as their occupation, source of income, and the purpose of the account. They are also responsible for ongoing monitoring of their customers' transactions and reporting any suspicious activities to regulatory authorities.

In addition to regulatory compliance, banks also benefit from KYC procedures as they help them to manage risk and prevent fraud. By knowing their customers, banks can better assess the risk of financial crime and take appropriate measures to mitigate it. They can also use KYC data to improve customer service and offer tailored financial products and services that meet their customers' needs. Overall, the role of banks in KYC is critical to ensuring the integrity and stability of the financial system.

Banks play a crucial role in KYC (Know Your Customer) because they are often the first point of contact for customers who want to open a new account, apply for a loan or conduct financial transactions. As part of their regulatory compliance, banks are required to collect and verify customer identification information to ensure that their services are not being used for fraudulent or criminal activities.

By conducting proper KYC, banks can identify and authenticate their customers, assess their risks, and monitor their transactions to detect any suspicious activity. This helps to prevent money laundering, terrorist financing, and other financial crimes.

Furthermore, banks are typically held responsible for any financial losses resulting from fraudulent or criminal activities conducted through their systems. Proper KYC helps to mitigate these risks and protect both the bank and its customers. Therefore, the role of banks in KYC is critical to maintaining the integrity and stability of the financial system.

LIMITATIONS IN IMPLEMENTING KYC IN INDIA

Despite its benefits, implementing KYC norms in India faces several challenges, including:

- Lack of infrastructure: India's vast population and geographic diversity present challenges for implementing a uniform KYC framework across the country.
- Limited access to identification documents: Many individuals in India do not have identification documents such as Aadhaar cards or passports, making it difficult for them to access financial services that require KYC verification.
- Limited awareness: Many individuals in India are not aware of KYC norms and their importance in preventing financial crimes, which can lead to non-compliance.

- Fraudulent Practices: Some individuals and entities in India engage in fraudulent practices to bypass KYC norms, such as using fake identification documents or providing false information.

PML AMENDMENTS IN 2023

The 2023 Amendments to the Know Your Customer (KYC) and Anti-Money Laundering (AML) regulations in India have introduced significant changes that aim to strengthen the framework for combating money laundering and terrorist financing. These amendments address various aspects, including group-wide policies, non-profit organizations, politically exposed persons, beneficial ownership, and virtual digital assets. In this post, we will analyze the provisions and their impact on reporting entities and businesses.

Here are some important amendments in the Prevention of Money Laundering Regulations.

GROUP-WIDE POLICIES

Under the amended rules, financial groups are required to implement group-wide policies to discharge their obligations under Chapter IV of the Prevention of Money Laundering Act, 2002. This aligns with FATF Recommendation No. 18, which emphasizes the importance of internal controls and programs against money laundering and terrorist financing at the group level. The purpose of these policies is to facilitate the reporting entity in meeting its obligations and managing risks associated with group entities.

Actionable: Reporting entities should identify the constituents of their group and formulate a group-wide policy that enables the discharge of obligations. The policy should align with

FATF guidance and include measures such as sharing information for customer due diligence and risk management.

NON-PROFIT ORGANIZATIONS (NPOS)

The government has made changes to the rules related to the law against money laundering. These changes require banks and financial institutions to gather information about the financial activities of non-profit organizations (NGOs) under the Prevention of Money Laundering Act (PMLA).

Additionally, financial institutions must register details of their NGO clients on the Darpan portal of the NITI Aayog (a government agency) and keep the records for five years after the business relationship ends or the account is closed. These records may also need to be shared with the Enforcement Directorate upon request.

The new rules state that banks and financial institutions must register the details of their NGO clients on the NITI Aayog's Darpan portal and maintain these records for five years after the relationship with the client ends. This registration process helps create a database of basic information about all NGOs.

The definition of a non-profit organization has also been updated to include entities or organizations established for religious or charitable purposes under the Income Tax Act. This includes trusts, societies registered under state legislation, and companies registered under the Companies Act.

Companies dealing with NPOs should ensure the registration of clients on the DARPAN Portal and maintain registration records as per the specified duration. Existing NPO clients should also be brought under the registration requirement through a defined mechanism and timeline.

POLITICALLY EXPOSED PERSONS (PEPS)

The definition of PEPs in the KYC Directions has been aligned with the PML Rules. PEPs include individuals entrusted with prominent public functions by foreign countries, such as heads of states or governments, senior politicians, government officers, and important political party officials. The amended definitions introduced the concept of Foreign PEPs.

As the definition of PEPs remains the same, reporting entities should continue following the existing provisions for identifying and verifying PEPs. Riskpro offers a separate certification course on the subject of PEPs. It is one of the most complicated subjects when the compliance officers dig deeper.

BENEFICIAL OWNERSHIP

The amended rules revise the threshold for determining beneficial ownership. For companies, beneficial owners are natural persons with controlling ownership interest exceeding 10% of shares, capital, or profits. In the case of trusts, beneficial ownership includes authors, trustees, beneficiaries with a 10% or higher interest, and individuals exercising ultimate effective control.

Reporting entities need to consider the revised limit of 10% for companies and trusts while determining beneficial ownership. This information should be incorporated into the KYC Policy and Standard Operating Procedures (SOP) of the reporting entity.

ADDITIONAL DOCUMENTATION

The amendments introduce additional document requirements for client due diligence. Companies need to submit certified copies of documents, including the names of relevant persons holding senior management positions. Partnership firms need to provide certified copies of partner names and registered office details. Trusts must submit certified copies of beneficiary names, trustees, settlor, and author details.

Reporting entities should update their KYC Policy and SOP to include the additional documents required for companies, partnership firms, and trusts. These documents should be collected and verified during the customer due diligence process.

VIRTUAL DIGITAL ASSETS (VDAS)

The amendment refers to the identification of specific activities involving virtual digital assets, such as exchanges, transfers, safekeeping, and providing financial services, as designated businesses or professions under the Prevention of Money Laundering Act, 2002. This designation implies that entities involved in these activities with virtual digital assets are now required to adhere to Know Your Customer (KYC) and Anti-Money Laundering (AML) regulations.

With this amendment, entities engaged in the mentioned activities must implement robust KYC procedures to verify the identities of their customers. This includes collecting relevant identification documents, conducting due diligence checks, and verifying the legitimacy of the customers' transactions.

Additionally, entities must also implement AML measures to detect and prevent money laundering and other illicit activities. This involves implementing transaction monitoring systems, reporting suspicious transactions to the relevant authorities, and maintaining comprehensive records of customer transactions.

Actionable: Reporting entities involved in virtual digital asset activities should ensure compliance with the designated business or profession requirements. This includes implementing robust KYC procedures, conducting customer due diligence, and reporting suspicious transactions to the appropriate authorities.

RECORD KEEPING AND REPORTING

On 7th March, 2023, Government of India notified the 2023 Amendment to the Prevention of Money-laundering (Maintenance of Records) Rules, 2005.

The amendments reinforce the importance of maintaining records and reporting suspicious transactions. Reporting entities are required to maintain records of transactions, including customer identification data and transactions of a specified value, for a minimum of ten years. Additionally, entities must submit a suspicious transaction report (STR) to the Financial Intelligence Unit-India (FIU-IND) within seven working days of identifying a suspicious transaction or providing information about it.

Actionable: Reporting entities should review their record-keeping practices to ensure compliance with the extended retention period of ten years. It is essential to have a robust system in place for recording and storing transaction data.

Additionally, reporting entities should establish efficient processes for identifying and reporting suspicious transactions to the FIU-IND within the specified timeframe.

THE INCLUSION OF PRACTICING PROFESSIONALS

The Central Government's notification dated 3rd May 2023 has amended the PMLA guidelines to include practicing CA/CS/CMA as persons carrying on designated business or profession. This move emphasizes the need for enhanced scrutiny and accountability for professionals involved in financial transactions related to activities such as buying and selling immovable property, managing client money and assets, handling bank accounts, organizing contributions for companies, and managing business entities. [iii]

Implications of the Amendment

- Compliance Requirements: Practicing professionals are now classified as "Reporting Entities" and are subject to various obligations under the PMLA. They must verify the identity of their clients, maintain records of transactions, and conduct enhanced due diligence to examine ownership, financial position, and sources of funds of their clients.
- Fines and Penalties: Failure to comply with PMLA obligations may result in monetary penalties imposed by the Director. The amendment stipulates penalties ranging from ten thousand rupees to one lakh rupees for each violation.
- Legal Immunity: Reporting entities, including practicing professionals, are granted immunity from civil or criminal proceedings for complying with their

obligations and furnishing information under the PMLA.

Rationale and Analysis

The inclusion of practicing CA/CS/CMA under the PMLA guidelines is a well-thought-out move aligned with international standards, particularly those set by FATF. This amendment extends the accountability and regulatory scrutiny to these professionals, similar to independent legal professionals, accountants, and trust and company service providers globally. However, the exclusion of lawyers from this amendment has raised concerns within the practicing professional community.

These amendments have directly impacted the way the financial entities and other stakeholders do the business in India, Reserve Bank of India have already aligned itself with the changes in the regulations. These changes can be read in the relevant chapters discussing the KYC Regulatory Framework.

KYC METHODS PREVALENT IN INDIA

The KYC (Know Your Customer) process in India involves six main methods, which are Physical, eKYC, Digital, Video, Depository, and offline. These methods are the core of this study material and provide a comprehensive overview of how KYC is carried out in India.

Over time, these methods have evolved to become more streamlined, efficient, and convenient for customers. Each method has its own unique features and benefits, allowing customers to choose the one that best suits their needs and preferences.

Overall, these six methods form the backbone of India's KYC system and help ensure that financial institutions have the necessary information to prevent money laundering and other fraudulent activities.

TYPES OF KYC PROCESSES

The Banking and Finance sector offers various KYC methods to ensure financial inclusion and manage risk.

KYC METHODS PREVALENT IN INDIA

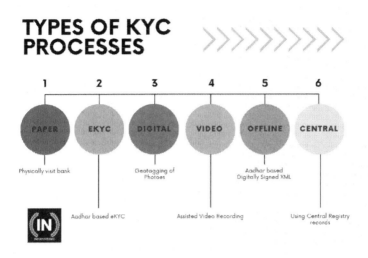

These include:

PAPER-BASED KYC

This type of verification requires submitting physical copies of address and identity proofs in person. Paper-based KYC is a type of Know Your Customer (KYC) verification process where a customer needs to physically visit a bank, fund house office, or KYC Registration Agency to complete the process. The customer needs to submit self-attested, physical copies of the required address and identity proofs, along with a signed KYC form. The KYC form and the documents are then verified by the concerned authorities to authenticate the customer's identity and address. This method of KYC verification is considered a traditional and more time-consuming process compared to other digital KYC methods available today.

The Indian law's KYC verification address proof requirements are not only inflexible but also excessively detailed. Indian regulators require customers to provide proof of multiple addresses, including current, permanent, and residence addresses. Unfortunately, this approach can create problems for marginalized or vulnerable groups, such as migrant laborers, nomadic communities, the homeless, and others who may not have a fixed or permanent address. Even in cases where individuals have a permanent address, they may not have the officially valid documents (OVDs) required to demonstrate their current address.

Moreover, the need for providing a current address can be problematic, even though pan-India identification schemes like Aadhaar, passports, and voter IDs exist. These documents are difficult to update and require proof of a local or current address, which may not always be easily accessible. For example, migrants working in the private or informal sector may not have a NREGA job card to use for address verification.

The strict requirements under Indian law can exacerbate the problem of financial exclusion, making it more difficult for these vulnerable groups to access financial services. As a result, regulators must work towards a more flexible and inclusive approach that accounts for the diverse circumstances of marginalized or vulnerable groups.

Steps in Paper Based KYC

Step 1: Download the KYC form from the website of the KYC Registration Agency, bank, or fund house where you wish to complete your KYC process.

Step 2: Fill in the required details in the form. You need to provide personal information like your name, address, date of birth, contact details, and other relevant information.

Step 3: Attach the physical, self-attested copies of the documents that serve as proof of your identity and address, like your Aadhaar card, passport, driving license, voter ID, or any other officially valid documents (OVDs) as per the KYC norms of the institution.

Step 4: Visit the bank, fund house office, or KYC Registration Agency office in person.

Step 5: Submit the signed KYC form along with the documents to an official present at the office.

Step 6: The official will verify the documents and process your KYC verification request. They may also take your photograph and biometric data, such as fingerprints and iris scans, for further verification.

Step 7: Once your documents are verified, the institution will update your KYC records in their database, and you will receive an acknowledgement receipt. This completes your paper-based KYC process.

The above steps outline the process for paper-based KYC. However, the process may differ slightly for other types of KYC. Here are the processes for some of the other types of KYC:

AADHAAR-BASED KYC

Aadhaar-based eKYC is a type of KYC verification that allows customers to verify their identity remotely using the data collected by the Unique Identification Authority of India (UIDAI) through Aadhaar OTP or biometric-based verification. In Aadhaar OTP-based verification, the customer provides their Aadhaar number and mobile number linked with their Aadhaar Card.

The OTP (One-Time Password) is then sent to the customer's mobile number, and the customer needs to enter the OTP in the provided field to complete the verification process. In biometric-based verification, the customer needs to provide their biometric information, which is evaluated using UIDAI-certified biometric scanners. This biometric information includes fingerprints and iris scans, which are unique to each individual and can be used to verify their identity. Using Aadhaar-based eKYC, customers can verify their identity remotely, without needing to physically visit the bank, fund house office, or KYC Registration Agency.

Overview of Aadhaar

Aadhaar is a unique identification number issued by the Unique Identification Authority of India (UIDAI) to Indian residents. The Aadhaar number serves as a proof of identity and address, based on the biometric and demographic information provided during the enrolment process. The Aadhaar card also includes a QR code that can be scanned to verify the authenticity of the document.

Aadhaar and KYC

In the financial sector, Aadhaar is used as a tool for Know Your Customer (KYC) verification. The Aadhaar-based KYC process enables remote authentication of customers, eliminating the need for physical verification. This process is faster and more convenient for customers, as it can be done from the comfort of their homes.

KYC METHODS PREVALENT IN INDIA

Aadhaar as a Primary Document for KYC

Aadhaar is considered a reliable and secure form of identification in India as it is a biometric-based identity proof that contains an individual's unique 12-digit identification number, along with their photograph, fingerprints, and iris scan. It is issued by the Unique Identification Authority of India (UIDAI), a statutory authority established under the Aadhaar Act 2016.

By allowing Aadhaar as a primary document for KYC, the Reserve Bank of India (RBI) and other regulatory authorities aim to simplify and streamline the KYC process for banks, financial institutions, and other regulated entities, as well as for customers. This helps in reducing the cost and time involved in the KYC process, enhancing the speed and efficiency of account opening, and promoting financial inclusion in the country.

Moreover, the use of Aadhaar for KYC purposes is also aligned with the Indian government's vision of a Digital India, where citizens can access services digitally and efficiently. With the Aadhaar-enabled KYC, customers can complete the KYC process remotely from the comfort of their homes or offices, using their mobile devices or computers. This also helps in reducing the need for physical documents and eliminates the risk of forgery or fraud, making the process more secure and reliable.

Digilocker and Aadhar KYC

DigiLocker is a service provided by the Indian government that helps people keep their important documents safe in a digital format. It's like a secure online storage where you can store documents like your Aadhaar card. DigiLocker also allows others to verify your identity using the electronic copy of your Aadhaar stored in DigiLocker.[iv]

Here's how Aadhaar-based verification through DigiLocker works:

- When you choose to verify using DigiLocker, you will be taken to a webpage recognized by UIDAI (Unique Identification Authority of India), which is the authority that issues Aadhaar cards.
- You will need to enter your Aadhaar number, followed by a One-Time Password (OTP) and a captcha. This is done to let the verifier service fetch the electronic copy of your Aadhaar from DigiLocker.
- Once the verifier has the electronic copy of your Aadhaar, they can verify your identity by comparing the information on the electronic copy with the information you provided.
- If the information matches, the organization can consider the verification process complete.

This method is efficient and secure because it eliminates the need for handling physical documents and reduces the chances of fraud. You can store your Aadhaar digitally in DigiLocker and easily share it with authorized organizations whenever they need to verify your identity.

Concerns and Issues Related to Aadhaar-based KYC

The use of Aadhaar for KYC verification has raised concerns regarding privacy and security. Some critics argue that the collection and storage of biometric information can be misused and lead to identity theft. The Supreme Court of India has also raised concerns regarding the mandatory linking of Aadhaar with various services and has set limits on the use of Aadhaar for KYC verification. The government has taken measures to address these concerns, such as implementing stricter regulations on the collection and use of Aadhaar data, and allowing customers to use other documents for KYC verification if they do not want to use Aadhaar.

The Financial Action Task Force (FATF) recommendations on Customer Due Diligence (CDD) do not mandate the adoption of a digital ID system for CDD procedures, and are technology-neutral. However, in 2017, the Indian government adopted Aadhaar as a digital ID for KYC purposes by mandating the linking of Aadhaar with bank accounts.

Puttuswamy Aadhar Test

The Puttaswamy Aadhaar test refers to a landmark judgment of the Supreme Court of India in 2018, in the case of K.S. Puttaswamy v. Union of India. The case was brought to challenge the constitutional validity of Aadhaar, a biometric identification system that was being used by the Indian government for various purposes, including for the purposes of KYC (Know Your Customer) verification by banks.

In its judgment, the Supreme Court held that the right to privacy is a fundamental right under the Indian Constitution, and that the use of Aadhaar must be subjected to strict scrutiny to ensure that it does not violate the right to privacy. The Court also struck down several provisions of the Aadhaar Act, including one that allowed private entities to use Aadhaar for verification purposes.

KYC METHODS PREVALENT IN INDIA

The Puttaswamy Aadhaar test essentially established a framework for evaluating the constitutionality of any law or policy that involves the collection, storage, and use of personal data in India. The test requires that any such law or policy must be supported by a legitimate state aim, must be proportionate to that aim, and must not result in the violation of the right to privacy.

The government re-introduced Aadhaar within the KYC banking framework as one of the many Officially Valid Documents (OVDs), such as passport and driving license, that could be used as identity and address proof, following the Supreme Court's decision. Banks and other notified FIs were permitted to verify the identity and address of the customer using Aadhaar-based eKYC authentication facility, offline verification under the Aadhaar Act, passport verification, or any other OVD such as PAN number or voter ID.

The re-introduction of Aadhaar has been justified by banks as being consensual and voluntary, and proponents point to the imperatives of financial inclusion and reducing authentication costs. However, there are concerns about whether a voluntary Aadhaar-based regime passes the Puttaswamy (II) (Aadhaar) test, which struck down Section 57 of the Aadhaar Act relating to the use of Aadhaar-based authentication by private parties on the ground that it would enable commercial exploitation of an individual's biometric and demographic information by the private entities.

There is also a de facto preference for Aadhaar-based eKYC authentication, even though it cannot be mandatory for participating in the banking system. KYC procedures while onboarding a customer also cannot insist on a customer

KYC METHODS PREVALENT IN INDIA

providing their Aadhaar number for authentication, verification, or as a residence or identity proof.

Steps involved in Aadhar Based eKYC

• Visit the website of the financial institution that offers Aadhaar-based eKYC. - This is the first step towards getting your eKYC done. Visit the official website of the financial institution that offers this service.

• Enter your Aadhaar number -Once you are on the website, enter your 12-digit Aadhaar number in the designated field. Make sure to double-check the number you entered before submitting it.

• Choose between OTP-based or biometric-based authentication - The next step is to choose between OTP-based or biometric-based authentication. For OTP-based verification, you will receive a One-Time Password (OTP) on your registered mobile number, which you will have to enter on the website. For biometric verification, you need to provide your biometrics, which would then be evaluated using UIDAI-certified biometric scanners.

• Enter the OTP or provide your biometrics - Depending on the option you choose in the previous step, you will either have to enter the OTP sent to your mobile number or provide your biometrics using UIDAI-certified biometric scanners.

• Submit the form - After successfully entering the OTP or providing your biometrics, submit the eKYC form on the website.

• The eKYC process will verify the details entered against the information on the Aadhaar database - The final step is where the eKYC process will verify the details entered against the information on the Aadhaar database. Once the verification is successful, you will receive a confirmation message or email from the financial institution.

DIGITAL KYC

Customers can upload scanned copies of KYC documents online and verify their identity through geotagged live photographs. Digital KYC is a method of verifying the identity of customers by allowing them to upload scanned copies of their KYC documents online. Along with this, the customer is required to provide a geotagged live photograph, which is a photograph with location information attached to it. This ensures that the customer is present at the location mentioned in the KYC documents. The digital KYC process then verifies the details entered against the information on the geotagged documents, allowing for a quicker and more convenient method of identity verification.

While both Digital KYC and eKYC allow for remote verification, the methods used for verification are different.

Digital KYC involves the geotagging of live photographs and scanned documents, while Aadhaar-based eKYC relies on the data collected by UIDAI and requires biometric verification or OTP-based verification.

Steps involved in Digital KYC

Step 1: Visit the website of the financial institution that offers digital KYC services. Look for the digital KYC option on the website and click on it.

Step 2: Once you click on the digital KYC option, you will be directed to a page where you can fill in your details. You will also be asked to upload the scanned copies of your KYC documents, such as your Aadhaar card, PAN card, or passport. Make sure that the scanned copies are clear and readable.

Step 3: After uploading the documents, you will be prompted to take a live photograph of yourself along with the OVDs, which include the KYC documents you uploaded. This photograph will be geotagged, which means that the location of the photograph will be recorded.

Step 4: Once you have submitted the form, the digital KYC process will verify the details you entered against the information on the geo-tagged documents. The process is automated and usually takes a few minutes. If the details match, your KYC verification will be successful, and you will receive a confirmation message from the financial institution. If there is any discrepancy, you may be asked to provide additional documents or visit the bank or financial institution in person for further verification.

OFFLINE KYC

Offline KYC is a type of KYC process that allows customers to provide their KYC details without being physically present or submitting physical copies of their documents. In the offline KYC process, the customer can download their Aadhaar Paperless Offline e-KYC document and share it with the financial institution.

Aadhaar Paperless Offline e-KYC is a digitally signed XML document containing the customer's KYC details, such as name, address, photograph, and Aadhaar number, among others. It can be generated by the customer from the UIDAI portal using their Aadhaar number and OTP authentication.

To complete the offline KYC process, the customer needs to provide their consent to the financial institution to use the Aadhaar Paperless Offline e-KYC document for verification purposes. Once the financial institution receives the document and the customer's consent, they can verify the KYC details against their records and complete the KYC process without the customer being physically present. This process saves time and effort for both the customer and the financial institution.

QR Based Aadhar Verification

According to the rules set by SEBI (Securities and Exchange Board of India), organizations responsible for verifying KYC (Know Your Customer) information, like CDSL (Central Depository Services Limited), can now independently confirm Aadhaar details. If you want to verify your identification, you can use the Aadhaar QR code in the following way:

- The organization will ask for your permission to collect your Aadhaar details.
- They will check if the QR code is visible and clear on your ID.
- They will scan the QR code to extract important information like your name, address, date of birth, and gender.
- They will hide the first eight digits of your Aadhaar number and the QR code itself (this is necessary) to protect your privacy.
- They will compare the information you provided with the data from Aadhaar to ensure it matches.

Verification using the QR code can be done through authorized channels' computer systems and is a cost-effective and reliable method for verifying IDs on a large scale, especially for fintech applications governed by SEBI.

XML Based Aadhar Verification

Aadhaar XML-based verification is a way to check a person's identity using a special file in a computer language called XML. This file contains the person's Aadhaar information like their name, address, and other details. When organizations want to confirm someone's identity, they compare the information in the XML file with what the person gave them during the verification process.

The people who manage Aadhaar (UIDAI) have rules that say their web pages can only be used on their own website. No other website is allowed to copy or recreate their pages or parts of them.

Aadhaar-XML process is simple and can be done entirely on the person's own device, like a computer or phone. Here are the steps:

• You will be taken to the UIDAI Offline XML page.
• You enter your Aadhaar Number and a security code called captcha, and then you get a one-time password (OTP).
• Once you log in, click on the 'Offline eKYC' option on the UIDAI website and create a special code for sharing.
• After your details are checked on the UIDAI page, the XML file is downloaded to your device.
• Finally, you have to manually upload the XML file on the verifier's website and enter the special sharing code you created earlier.

Aadhaar XML-based verification helps organizations automate the process of confirming someone's identity.

Instead of manually comparing the information provided by the person with their Aadhaar, they can use the information in the XML file. This reduces the chances of mistakes and makes the verification process more efficient.

Steps involved in Offline KYC

Go to the website of Unique Identification Authority of India (UIDAI) and download the Aadhaar Paperless Offline e-KYC document. This document contains all the necessary information about you that is required for KYC verification.

Fill in all the details requested in the Aadhaar Paperless Offline e-KYC document. Make sure that you fill in all the fields correctly and completely, as any errors may cause delays or rejections during the KYC verification process.

Once you have filled in all the details, share the document with the financial institution where you want to complete the KYC process. You can share the document by uploading it on the financial institution's website or by providing a physical copy to the institution.

When you share the document with the financial institution, you will also need to provide your consent that the information in the document can be used for KYC verification purposes.

After you have submitted the Aadhaar Paperless Offline e-KYC document and provided your consent, the financial institution will initiate the KYC verification process. They will cross-check the details in the document with the information in their database and verify your identity.

If your KYC verification is successful, you will be informed by the financial institution, and your KYC process will be considered complete. If there are any discrepancies or errors, the financial institution will inform you, and you may need to submit additional documents or rectify the errors before the verification process can be completed.

CENTRAL KYC

Central KYC or CKYC is a process in which the KYC documents and identity of a customer are verified, and the KYC records are added to a central repository. This central repository is maintained by the Central Registry of Securitisation Asset Reconstruction and Security Interest of India (CERSAI).[v]

Doing KYC every time you want to access a financial service can be inconvenient for both customers and businesses. To reduce this burden and prevent financial crimes, the Indian government introduced the CKYC system.

Central KYC, or CKYC, is an initiative by the government of India to make the KYC process the same across all financial institutions. It is overseen by CERSAI, a central registry. CKYC aims to make the process easier by storing customer information in one central location.

Before CKYC, customers had to go through a lot of paperwork when using financial services. With CKYC, this paperwork is eliminated. The data is securely stored digitally in a central repository. Authorized financial institutions can access this information, making it more convenient for both customers and banks.

Here are some key features of CKYC:

- KYC Identification Number (KIN): Each customer's KYC data is linked to a unique identifier called the KIN.
- Centralized Repository: The customer's data is stored digitally in one centralized location.
- Easy Access for Financial Institutions: Financial institutions can access KYC records in bulk by entering the customer's CKYC identifier, without the need for additional paperwork.
- Updated Records: When a customer's KYC records are updated, relevant organizations are notified.
- Multiple Correspondence Addresses: Customers can link their KYC to multiple addresses for convenience.

Constituents of CKYC Ecosystem

There are five main constituents of CKYC

- Central Registry of Securitisation and Asset Reconstruction (CERSAI): CERSAI is the central authority responsible for overseeing and maintaining the CKYC Registry. It acts as the repository for the KYC data of individuals and ensures the security and accessibility of the information.
- Financial Institutions (FIs): FIs refer to banks, insurance companies, mutual fund companies, and other entities in the financial services sector. These institutions are the primary users of the CKYC system. They rely on the centralized repository maintained by CERSAI to access and verify customer KYC information for various financial services.
- Registrars: Registrars are authorized entities that facilitate the onboarding of customers onto the CKYC platform. They collect the necessary KYC documents and details from customers, verify the information, and upload it to the CKYC

KYC METHODS PREVALENT IN INDIA

system. Registrars can be banks, insurance companies, or other entities appointed by CERSAI.

- KYC Registration Agencies (KRAs): KYC Registration Agencies are entities approved by the Securities and Exchange Board of India (SEBI) to carry out KYC verification processes. They play a crucial role in collecting and validating KYC data for individuals who wish to invest in the securities market. Some KRAs also participate in the CKYC process by sharing their verified KYC records with CERSAI.

- Unique Identification Authority of India (UIDAI): UIDAI is the government agency responsible for issuing Aadhaar cards, which are unique identification numbers assigned to Indian residents. Aadhaar is an essential component of KYC verification, and its database is used in the CKYC process to authenticate individuals' identities.

How does CKYC work?

When you want to avail a financial service in India, completing KYC is mandatory. With CKYC, you only need to complete KYC once. Here's how it works:

Fill out a KYC form provided by the financial institution where you want to invest or obtain services. This form is then sent to CERSAI for verification.

CERSAI checks if the guidelines for CKYC are followed and securely stores the KYC documents in one server.

Once your CKYC is successfully completed, you receive a 14-digit KYC Identification Number (KIN) via SMS and email. Your ID proof is linked to this number.

After completing CKYC, you can use the KIN to complete KYC with any other financial institution without submitting additional paperwork. Businesses can access your documents through CERSAI to verify your KYC.

Benefits of CKYC

- Simplified Process: CKYC simplifies the account opening process by eliminating the need for repeated KYC procedures.
- Cost Reduction: Financial institutions save costs by accessing the centralized KYC database, reducing the need for multiple KYC verifications.
- Time-saving: Customers don't have to go through the entire KYC process again. It also reduces the turnaround time for KYC verification.
- Fraud Prevention: CKYC helps prevent fraud and money laundering by standardizing the identification process and securing customer data.

Steps involved in CKYC

Central KYC (CKYC) is a process for submitting KYC documents and authenticating your identity. The process involves the following steps:

Step 1: Fill in the KYC form and provide the required KYC documents to a bank or financial institution that is registered with the KYC Registration Agency (KRA).

Step 2: The bank or financial institution will verify your KYC documents and authenticate your identity. Once verified, the KYC details are uploaded to the central repository maintained by the Central Registry of Securitisation Asset Reconstruction and Security Interest of India (CERSAI).

Step 3: The KYC records are added to the central repository, and a unique 14-digit identification number is assigned to the record. The central repository can be accessed by authorized entities such as banks, insurance companies, mutual funds, and other financial institutions for the purpose of KYC verification.

The CKYC process is designed to simplify the KYC process and make it more efficient by creating a central repository of KYC records that can be accessed by authorized entities. It also helps in reducing the burden of submitting KYC documents multiple times for different financial products and services. Once your KYC is completed through the CKYC process, you can use the same KYC details for various financial products and services across different financial institutions.

Consider an example of CKYC.

Suppose Mr. Sharma wants to open a new bank account with Bank A. In the past, Mr. Sharma would have had to provide various documents and complete the KYC process separately for Bank A, even if he had already completed KYC with another bank.

However, with the introduction of CKYC, the process becomes simpler. Mr. Sharma visits Bank A and expresses his intention to open an account. Instead of going through the entire KYC process again, Bank A asks Mr. Sharma if he has completed CKYC previously. If he has, Bank A requests his CKYC Identification Number (KIN).

Mr. Sharma shares his KIN, which is a unique 14-digit identifier associated with his KYC data. Bank A enters this KIN into the CKYC system and retrieves Mr. Sharma's KYC information from the centralized repository maintained by CERSAI.

The KYC information includes Mr. Sharma's identity proof, address proof, and other relevant details. Bank A verifies the retrieved information and completes the necessary checks to ensure compliance with KYC regulations. If everything is in order, Mr. Sharma's account is opened with Bank A without the need for additional paperwork or repeating the entire KYC process.

Later, if Mr. Sharma wants to open an investment account with a mutual fund company or apply for a loan with Bank B, he can simply provide his KIN. Bank B can use the KIN to access Mr. Sharma's KYC data from the CKYC system, eliminating the need for him to submit KYC documents again.

In this way, CKYC simplifies the process of availing financial services. It saves time and effort for both customers like Mr. Sharma and financial institutions like Bank A and Bank B. The centralized repository of KYC data ensures consistency and helps prevent fraudulent activities by maintaining accurate and verified customer information.

It's important to note that CKYC is designed to ensure data privacy and security. Only authorized financial institutions can access the KYC data, and strict measures are in place to protect the confidentiality of customer information.

VIDEO KYC

Video KYC is a type of KYC (Know Your Customer) verification process that enables individuals to complete the KYC process entirely online without the need for physical documents. In the video KYC process, the customer is required to record a video of themselves, which is submitted to a financial institution for verification. The process can be either assisted or non-assisted, but it is entirely paperless and online.

During the video KYC process, the customer is required to provide details about their identity and other relevant information. The video recording is then reviewed by an agent from the financial institution, who verifies the information provided by the customer against their government-issued identity documents.

The video KYC process is aimed at making the KYC process more convenient for customers and reducing the need for in-person verification. It can be particularly useful for customers who are unable to visit a bank branch or who live in remote areas. The process also provides greater security against fraud, as the verification is done by a trained agent who can spot inconsistencies in the information provided by the customer.

Here is the summary of requirements by Reserve Bank of India about Video KYC process.

- The Registered Entity should follow the RBI guidelines on resilience framework for banks, minimum baseline cyber security, and general IT risks. The V-CIP's technology infrastructure should be housed in the RE's premises. Also, its connection and interaction should originate from the RE's secured network domain. If the RE decides to outsource any technology-related processes, it must comply with the relevant RBI guidelines.

- The RE must follow appropriate encryption standards and ensure end-to-end data encryption between customer device & hosting. The customer consent recording must be auditable and alteration-proof.
- The V-CIP must be able to detect IP addresses from outside India or IP spoofing and prevent connection with the same.
- The video recording should be geo-tagged (containing live GPS coordinates of the customer) and have a date-time stamp. The live video quality in the V-CIP must be clear enough for a doubtless identification of the customer.
- Even though the responsibility of customer identification lies with the RE, the V-CIP must be able to detect face liveness and spoofing and also conduct a face match. REs can use appropriate artificial intelligence (AI) technology to ensure a robust V-CIP.
- Based on experience with forged identity cases, the V-CIPs technology infrastructure, application software, and workflows must be regularly updated. Any case of forged identity should be reported as a cyber event under exact regulatory guidelines.
- To ensure the V-CIP's robustness & encryption capabilities, it must undergo tests such as Vulnerability Assessment, Penetration testing, and Security Audit. These tests must be run periodically (as per internal/regulatory guidelines) and conducted by suitably accredited agencies as prescribed by the RBI. Any critical issues found during testing must be resolved before implementation.

- The functional, performance, and maintenance strength of the V-CIP application and APIs must be tested before being used in a live environment. These tests must be run periodically (as per internal/regulatory guidelines). Any critical issues found during testing must be resolved before implementation.
- The Registered Entity must create a clear workflow and standard operating procedure for Video Based KYC and adhere to it. Next, the Video Based KYC process must be operated only by specially trained officials of the Registered Entity. This official should be capable of conducting liveliness checks, detecting fraudulent attempts, and acting upon them.
- If Video KYC process is disrupted due to some reason, it should be aborted and a fresh session should be started.
- The sequence and/or the type of security questions (including those that indicate the liveness of the customer) during the video call should be varied to ensure real-time interaction and the absence of per-recording.
- On detection of any prompting at the customer's end, the Registered Entity must reject the account opening process.
- Details about the customer undergoing Video Based KYC – like if they are new or existing, had been rejected before, or their name appears in some negative list – should be considered at an appropriate stage of the Video KYC workflow.

- The official of the Registered Entity (one who is conducting the V-CIP) must record the audio-visual and capture a photograph of the customer during the video call for identification. Further, they must obtain identification information using any of the below ways:
    - OTP-based Aadhaar e-KYC authentication
    - Offline Verification of Aadhaar for identification
    - KYC records downloaded from CKYCR, following Section 56, using the KYC identifier provided by the customer
    - Equivalent e-document of Officially Valid Documents (OVDs) including documents issued through Digilocker
    - Registered Entity must redact or blackout the Aadhaar number in terms of Section 16.

Digilocker and Video KYC

Before we go to understand how Digilocker is used in Video Based KYC process, let us first see what is DigiLocker. So, Digilocker offers a cloud-based storage facility where users can upload, store, and share various types of documents, including identity proofs, educational certificates, vehicle registration documents, and more.

When it comes to the Know Your Customer (KYC) process, Digilocker can be helpful in several ways as it has two important characteristics viz. its held in secured cloud server and its authenticated by the Government.

- Document Storage: Users can upload their KYC documents, such as Aadhaar card, PAN card, driving license, voter ID, and passport, to their Digilocker account. This eliminates the need to carry physical copies of these documents and provides a convenient and secure digital alternative.
- Verification and Authentication: Digilocker integrates with various government agencies and departments to facilitate the verification and authentication of documents. Organizations that require KYC verification can access these documents directly from Digilocker with the user's consent, ensuring the authenticity and validity of the provided information.
- Paperless Process: By digitizing the KYC process, Digilocker reduces the reliance on paper documents. This not only saves time but also contributes to environmental sustainability by reducing paper waste.

Besides this, Digilocker is very helpful tool in the Video Based Customer Identification process.

The video KYC process mandated by the Reserve Bank of India (RBI) and Securities and Exchange Board of India (SEBI) can only accept ID documents that have been authenticated using the e-Sign facility provided by the DigiLocker system, as per Indian law. This means that customers without a DigiLocker account are unable to complete the video KYC process, thereby creating a barrier to access for those individuals. Moreover, the requirement to have a DigiLocker account can be an additional challenge for customers since only Aadhaar holders can create a DigiLocker account.

In addition, the video KYC process requires a bank official to conduct the video call in real-time, which can be resource-intensive and limit scaling. Therefore, implementation of the video KYC process can be problematic for the digital divide.

Video Based Customer Identification

Customer Due Diligence (CDD) is an essential process in financial institutions (FIs) to prevent money laundering and terrorist financing. As part of CDD, FIs must not only collect information on customers but also authenticate their identity. Traditionally, this process involved face-to-face transactions where customers filled out forms and provided identification documents to the bank. However, in recent years, FIs have moved towards digital authentication methods such as Video-based Customer Identification Process (V-CIP) and Aadhaar-based eKYC.

V-CIP is a new face-to-face full KYC process introduced by the Reserve Bank of India (RBI) in 2020, which allows customers to open new bank accounts remotely without physically interacting with bank officials. It requires customers to provide their personal details, specifically Aadhaar and PAN, which the bank then records videos and captures photographs for identification purposes. The live location of the customers is also captured via geo-tagging to ensure they are physically present in India. Banks may use additional verification processes and conduct concurrent audits to ensure the integrity of the process.

However, the catch with V-CIP is that while it requires users to provide their "informed consent," customers must provide their Aadhaar to access this service. As per the RBI's Master Circular, banks only have the option of using OTP-based

Aadhaar eKYC authentication or offline verification of Aadhaar for V-CIP identification.

Requesting entities, other than banks, are only permitted to carry out offline verification of Aadhaar for identification. As a result, customers can only access Video KYC (or V-CIP) if they use their Aadhaar number, which goes against the spirit of the Supreme Court's judgement in Puttaswamy (II)(Aadhaar) that struck down mandatory e-KYC Aadhaar-based authentication or bank linking.

While V-CIP and other digital forms of KYC have witnessed an upsurge in popularity during the Covid-19 pandemic, it is essential to balance customer convenience with privacy, autonomy, and choice. FIs must implement proper safeguards to ensure the authenticity and integrity of the authentication process while respecting the fundamental right to privacy of customers.

Steps involved in Video KYC

Video KYC is a convenient and paperless method of completing your KYC verification online. The following are the steps to avail of the video KYC service:

Step 1: Go to the website or app of the financial institution offering video KYC. You can find this information on their official website or by contacting their customer support.

Step 2: Once you have accessed the video KYC service, you need to submit your KYC documents and record a video using the web portal or app provided by the financial institution. The video recording will typically include your introduction, showing your face and KYC documents, and answering some verification questions.

Step 3: After you have submitted the video, the application will be manually reviewed and verified by an authorized agent to ensure fraud-free authentication. Once the verification is complete, you will be notified of the status of your KYC verification.

It is essential to note that the video KYC process may differ slightly depending on the financial institution offering the service. However, the basic steps outlined above are common to most video KYC verification processes.

IDENTIFICATION DOCUMENTS REQUIRED FOR KYC

In KYC (Know Your Customer) procedures, identification documents are required to verify the identity of a customer or client. These documents are used to establish the identity of an individual, and to ensure that the information provided by them is accurate and up to date.

The types of identification documents that are required for KYC purposes may vary depending on the jurisdiction, the nature of the business, and the risk profile of the customer. In general, however, the following documents are commonly accepted as forms of identification:

- Passport: A passport is a government-issued document that is used for international travel. It typically contains a photograph, name, date of birth, nationality, and signature of the holder.
- National ID card: A national identity card is a government-issued document that is used to establish the identity of a citizen or resident of a country. It typically contains a photograph, name, date of birth, and other identifying information. The national ID of

India is the Aadhaar card, which is a 12-digit unique identification number issued by the Unique Identification Authority of India (UIDAI). The Aadhaar card is considered as a valid proof of identity and address throughout India and is used in various government and private sector services for verification purposes.
- Driver's license: A driver's license is a government-issued document that is used to establish the identity of a driver. It typically contains a photograph, name, date of birth, and address of the holder.
- Voter ID card: A voter ID card is a government-issued document that is used to establish the identity of a voter. It typically contains a photograph, name, date of birth, and address of the holder.
- PAN card: A PAN (Permanent Account Number) card is a government-issued document that is used to establish the identity of a taxpayer. It typically contains a photograph, name, and unique identification number of the holder.

In addition to these documents, some organizations may also require additional documentation to verify the identity of a customer or client, such as utility bills or bank statements. The purpose of these additional documents is to establish the address of the customer or client and to ensure that they are a legitimate account holder.

ADDRESS PROOF DOCUMENTS REQUIRED FOR KYC

Address proof, in the context of KYC (Know Your Customer), refers to a document or evidence provided by an individual to establish and verify their residential address. It is a document that demonstrates the individual's current address and is required by financial institutions and other businesses as part of the KYC process.

The purpose of address proof is to ensure that the individual's stated address is accurate and can be verified. It helps in establishing the identity and residential address of the customer, which is essential for various financial transactions and services.

Address proof documents typically include government-issued identification cards, utility bills, bank statements, or any other official documents that display the individual's name and residential address. These documents should be recent and usually within the last three months to ensure their relevance and accuracy.

By providing a valid address proof, individuals help financial institutions and businesses comply with regulatory requirements, prevent fraud, and ensure the legitimacy and traceability of transactions.

The following documents can also be used as proof of address other than the four main documents mentioned earlier.

- Registered Agreement for Lease or Sale of Residence
- Utility bills not older than three months
- Bank account statement not older than 3 months
- Self-declaration validating the address offered by a High Court or Supreme Court judge
- Address proof issued by bank managers of Multinational Foreign Banks, Scheduled Commercial Banks and Scheduled Co-Operative Banks

- Address proof issued by a central/state government department, or any of the statutory or regulatory bodies
- ID card with address issued to members by professional bodies such as ICAI, ICSI, Bar Council, etc.
- Land or municipal tax receipt
- Monthly pension payment records issued by ministries or public sector companies that have the address mentioned.

KYC FOR DIFFERENT INDUSTRIES

The Know Your Customer (KYC) process is being widely adopted across various industries where customer identification and verification are of utmost importance. Banking and financial services are at the forefront, as they are legally obligated to verify customer identities to prevent financial crimes. KYC helps banks assess customer risks, maintain regulatory compliance, and uphold the integrity of the financial system. Insurance companies also rely on KYC procedures to verify policyholders and beneficiaries, ensuring accurate underwriting and preventing fraudulent claims. Securities brokers and investment service providers adopt KYC to meet regulatory obligations, identifying investors, preventing insider trading, and promoting transparency in financial markets. The rise of fintech has further emphasized the need for KYC, as digital banking, payment services, and lending platforms must verify customer identities and comply with anti-money laundering regulations.

The impact of KYC extends beyond traditional financial sectors. E-commerce platforms and online marketplaces utilize KYC verification for sellers and vendors, fostering trust, protecting consumers from fraud, and creating a secure online shopping environment. Telecommunications companies in certain regions must perform KYC processes to verify the identities of customers acquiring SIM cards or subscribing to their services, preventing misuse and ensuring compliance. Even the healthcare industry leverages KYC for patient registration, particularly in cases involving insurance claims and government-funded healthcare programs, safeguarding against identity theft and fraudulent activities. In the travel and hospitality sector, implementing KYC procedures is vital to comply with immigration and security regulations, prevent identity fraud, and ensure passenger safety. The real estate industry, in select jurisdictions, also adopts KYC to combat money laundering in high-value property transactions, verifying the identities of buyers, sellers, and other involved parties.

In essence, any industry involving financial transactions, customer onboarding, or regulatory compliance can benefit from implementing the KYC process. KYC not only establishes the authenticity of customers but also promotes trust, security, and regulatory compliance across a wide range of sectors.

KYC IN BANKING AND FINANCIAL SERVICES

Financial institutions are subject to robust KYC requirements due to the nature of their services, which involve managing and transacting large amounts of money on behalf of their customers. Here are some key elements of KYC in financial institutions:

PERSONAL INFORMATION

Financial institutions collect and verify personal information of their customers, including full name, date of birth, residential address, contact details, and national identification numbers. This information helps establish the customer's identity and serves as the basis for further verification.

IDENTIFICATION DOCUMENTS

Customers are required to provide official identification documents such as passports, national identity cards, driver's licenses, or any other government-issued identification. These documents are used to validate the customer's identity and cross-check against the information provided.

PROOF OF ADDRESS

Financial institutions typically require customers to provide proof of address, such as utility bills (electricity, water, gas), bank statements, rental agreements, or government-issued documents that display the customer's name and residential address. This helps ensure that the customer's stated address is accurate and can be verified.

FINANCIAL RECORDS

Financial institutions may request financial records, such as income statements, tax returns, bank statements, or investment portfolios, to gain insights into the customer's financial background and assess their financial activities.

POLITICALLY EXPOSED PERSONS (PEPS)

Financial institutions are required to conduct enhanced due diligence on customers who are classified as politically exposed persons (PEPs). PEPs are individuals who hold prominent public positions or have close associations with public officials. These customers are considered higher risk due to the potential for corruption or illicit activities.

SANCTION LISTS AND ADVERSE MEDIA SCREENING

Financial institutions perform screenings against global sanction lists and adverse media databases to identify if a customer is involved in any illegal activities, terrorism financing, or money laundering. This helps institutions comply with anti-money laundering (AML) regulations and prevent illicit transactions.

ONGOING MONITORING

Financial institutions have an obligation to monitor customer accounts and transactions on an ongoing basis. This involves periodic reviews to ensure that customer information remains up to date and to detect any suspicious or unusual activities.

KYC IN TELECOM

When you want to get a new mobile connection or avail of services from a telecommunications company, they will ask you for some information to verify who you are. This includes providing your personal details like your full name, date of birth, and address. They will also ask you to provide documents like your identification card, passport, or driver's license to prove your identity.

The telecommunications company will then check the information you provided against the documents you submitted to make sure everything matches up. They want to be sure that you are who you say you are. In some cases, they may also ask for additional proof of address, like a utility bill or a bank statement, to confirm your residential address.

IDENTITY FRAUD

The telecommunications industry is particularly vulnerable to identity fraud due to its extensive customer base, reliance on digital platforms, and the sensitive nature of customer information it holds. Criminals exploit weaknesses in security systems, such as weak authentication processes or inadequate safeguards for customer data, to carry out their fraudulent schemes.

The consequences of identity fraud in the telecommunications industry are far-reaching. Not only does it result in financial losses for both customers and service providers, but it also tarnishes the reputation of telecom companies, erodes customer trust, and can lead to legal repercussions. Furthermore, identity fraud can disrupt essential services, compromise personal privacy, and even facilitate other criminal activities, such as telecommunications-related scams or identity theft.

To combat identity fraud, telecom companies must prioritize robust security measures, stringent customer verification processes, and continuous monitoring of suspicious activities.

EKYC IN TELECOM

eKYC, or electronic Know Your Customer, is of utmost importance in the telecom industry. It plays a crucial role in verifying the identities of customers and ensuring the integrity of their information. The paragraphs below provide further insights:

In the telecommunications sector, where services are often provided remotely and online, the traditional process of verifying customer identities through physical documents and face-to-face interactions is not always feasible or efficient. This is where eKYC steps in, offering a digital and streamlined approach to customer identification.

eKYC enables telecom companies to authenticate the identities of their customers using electronic means, such as digital documents and biometric data. It simplifies the onboarding process for customers by eliminating the need for extensive paperwork and in-person visits to service centers.

By adopting eKYC methods, telecom companies can verify customer identities swiftly and securely. This helps prevent instances of identity fraud, where individuals use false or stolen identities to obtain telecom services illicitly. eKYC ensures that only legitimate customers are granted access to services, protecting both the telecom company and its genuine customers from potential risks and fraudulent activities.

eKYC also offers convenience and efficiency to customers. They can provide their identification details electronically, eliminating the need for physical documents and reducing the time and effort required to complete the verification process. This digital approach aligns with the increasingly digital lifestyles of customers and enhances their overall experience with the telecom provider.

eKYC helps telecom companies in maintaining compliance with regulatory requirements. Governments and regulatory bodies often mandate strict guidelines for customer identification and verification to combat fraud, money laundering, and other illicit activities. eKYC provides a reliable and standardized method for meeting these regulatory obligations, ensuring that telecom companies adhere to the prescribed norms.

eKYC is essential in the telecom industry as it enables efficient and secure verification of customer identities, helps prevent identity fraud, enhances customer convenience, and ensures compliance with regulatory requirements. By embracing eKYC, telecom companies can streamline their operations, protect their customers, and maintain the trust and integrity of their services.

BIOMETRIC VERIFICATION

In the telecommunications industry, e-KYC serves the purpose of verifying the authenticity of the documents provided by customers during the onboarding process. However, traditional methods of document verification may not always be fool proof, as forged or stolen documents can be used to deceive the system. Biometric KYC addresses this issue by incorporating biometric technology to ensure that the person providing the documents is the rightful owner.

By utilizing biometric technology, such as fingerprints, voice recognition, iris scanning, or facial recognition, telecom companies can verify the identity of customers with a high level of accuracy. Biometric traits are unique to individuals, making them difficult to replicate or manipulate. This robust security measure helps in preventing identity fraud and ensures that only genuine customers are granted access to telecom services.

In addition to verifying identity, biometric KYC also enables telecom operators to evaluate the risks associated with customers through various checks. By analyzing biometric data, such as facial features or voice patterns, telecom companies can assess the credibility and trustworthiness of customers. This helps in identifying potential risks and preventing fraudulent activities, ultimately safeguarding the interests of both the telecom company and its legitimate customers.

The use of biometric technology in KYC procedures offers several advantages. Firstly, it provides enhanced security compared to traditional methods reliant on passwords or PINs, as biometric traits are unique and difficult to replicate. Secondly, it simplifies the user experience by eliminating the need for customers to remember and manage complex passwords. Biometric authentication is convenient and user-friendly, making it easier for customers to comply with the verification process.

By implementing biometric KYC, telecom companies can strengthen their security measures and reduce the occurrence of identity fraud. Biometric technology adds an extra layer of protection by utilizing the unique biological traits of individuals, ensuring that only genuine customers are granted access to telecom services. This not only enhances security but also instils confidence among customers, as they can trust that their personal information is being handled securely by the telecom company.

Biometric KYC is a valuable tool in preventing identity fraud in the telecommunications industry. Its use of biometric technology provides robust security, simplifies the user experience, and helps telecom companies assess customer risks. By leveraging biometric authentication, telecom operators can significantly mitigate the risks associated with identity fraud, ensuring a safer and more secure environment for both the industry and its customers.

REGULATORY FRAMEWORK

In India, telecommunications companies are bound by legal and regulatory frameworks concerning KYC (Know Your Customer). These frameworks are designed to prevent the misuse of services for illegal activities like terrorism financing, money laundering, or fraud.

Telecom Regulatory Authority of India (TRAI) Guidelines: The TRAI sets guidelines and regulations for telecommunications companies operating in India. These guidelines include provisions for KYC compliance to ensure the integrity and security of the telecom services provided.

• Aadhaar-based KYC: The Unique Identification Authority of India (UIDAI) has introduced Aadhaar-based e-KYC for telecommunications services. It allows customers to verify their identities using their Aadhaar number, a unique identification number issued by the UIDAI. This process streamlines and simplifies the KYC procedure for both customers and telecom operators.

• Customer Identity Verification: Telecommunications companies are required to verify the identity of customers by collecting relevant personal information, such as full name, address, date of birth, and Aadhaar number or any other acceptable identification documents.

- Address Verification: Along with identity verification, telecom companies also verify the residential address of customers. This helps ensure that the provided address is accurate and can be validated.
- Document Retention: Telecom companies are obligated to retain the KYC documents provided by customers for a specified period as per regulatory requirements. This is done to comply with record-keeping obligations and facilitate audits or investigations, if necessary.
- Periodic Re-verification: As part of the ongoing KYC process, telecom operators may conduct periodic re-verification of customer details to ensure the accuracy and currency of customer information.
- Compliance Monitoring: Regulatory authorities, such as the Department of Telecommunications (DoT), monitor the compliance of telecom companies with KYC regulations. Non-compliance may result in penalties or other enforcement actions.

By adhering to these legal and regulatory frameworks, Indian telecommunications companies contribute to the national efforts in curbing illegal activities, protecting national security, and maintaining the integrity of the telecom sector. KYC requirements help ensure that the services are used by legitimate customers and discourage misuse for unlawful purposes.

KYC IN INSURANCE

KYC is equally important for insurance companies as it ensures the authenticity of investments and insurance policies. It ensures that insurance coverage is received by the rightful policyholders and helps in proper tax compliance. The

IRDAI plays a crucial role in setting guidelines and regulations to ensure the integrity and stability of the insurance industry. On 1st August 2022, the IRDAI introduced a new set of regulations specifically aimed at safeguarding the insurance sector against money laundering.

While similar standards for KYC and AML have long been in place for life insurance companies, these new regulations mark the first time that general insurers are subjected to stringent onboarding rules. This expansion of regulatory requirements reflects the growing importance of combating money laundering and ensuring the integrity of the insurance sector as a whole.

By implementing these guidelines, the IRDAI aims to enhance transparency, strengthen the financial system, and protect policyholders and other stakeholders from potential risks associated with money laundering. The mandatory nature of performing KYC and AML checks underscores the commitment of the IRDAI to uphold the highest standards of integrity and security in the insurance industry.

KYC PROCESSES ACCEPTED BY IRDAI

The Insurance Regulatory and Development Authority of India (IRDAI) has approved various KYC processes that insurers can adopt. These processes ensure proper customer identification and verification in the insurance sector. The accepted KYC methods by IRDAI are as follows:

- Aadhaar-based KYC through online authentication: Insurers can verify customers' identities by authenticating their Aadhaar details online. This process involves validating the Aadhaar information provided by the customer against the Aadhaar database.

- Aadhaar-based KYC through offline authentication: In this method, insurers can verify customer identities by conducting offline authentication of Aadhaar documents. The customer's Aadhaar details are manually verified and validated against the physical Aadhaar card provided by the customer.
- Digital KYC as per PML Rules: Insurers can comply with the Prevention of Money Laundering (PML) rules by using digital KYC methods. This involves collecting and verifying customer details electronically, following the prescribed PML guidelines.
- Video-Based Identification Process (VBIP): Insurers have the option to conduct video-based identification of customers. This process allows customers to undergo identity verification through a video call with the insurer.
- Using the 'KYC identifier' allotted by the CKYCR: Insurers can utilize the KYC identifier provided by the Central KYC Registry (CKYCR) to verify customer identities. The CKYCR serves as a centralized repository of KYC data, and insurers can access customer information using the unique KYC identifier.
- Using the customer's Officially Valid Documents (OVD): Insurers can also perform KYC using the customer's officially valid documents. These documents may include government-issued identification such as Aadhaar, PAN card, voter ID, passport, or driving license. Insurers validate the customer's identity by verifying the details mentioned in the provided OVDs.

By adopting these approved KYC processes, insurers can ensure compliance with IRDAI regulations and establish the authenticity of their customers. These methods enable a streamlined and secure KYC verification process in the insurance industry, promoting transparency and safeguarding against fraud.

KYC FOR INDIVIDUAL CUSTOMERS

he Insurance Regulatory and Development Authority of India (IRDAI) has established guidelines for insurers to conduct customer KYC in a specific manner. The requirements differ for individual customers and juridical persons (entities). Here is the step-by-step guide for the individual customers.

- True Identity Determination: Insurers must make their best efforts to determine the true identity of individual customers.
- Special Procedures: Insurers should have special procedures in place to identify both new and existing customers effectively.
- Avoidance of Anonymous or Fictitious Names: Insurers must ensure that no insurance contracts are given to individuals with anonymous or fictitious names.
- Identity, Address, and Photograph Verification: Insurers should verify the identity, address, and recent photograph of the customer.
- Address Self-Declaration: If a customer wants to submit an address different from what is mentioned on their Aadhaar card (a unique identification number), insurers may ask for a self-declaration. Otherwise, Aadhaar can serve as both identity and address proof.

- OVD Request: In cases where customers cannot go through Aadhaar authentication due to reasons such as age, injury, illness, or other factors, insurers may request Officially Valid Documents (OVD) to verify the customer's identity.

KYC FOR JURIDICAL PERSONS

Entity and Beneficial Owner Identification: Insurers must take steps to identify the entity and its beneficial owner(s) in the case of juridical persons.

- Beneficial Ownership Verification: Insurers should take reasonable steps to identify the beneficial ownership of the entity. Beneficial ownership refers to a natural person who ultimately owns or controls the entity on whose behalf the transaction is being conducted.
- Authorization Verification: Insurers need to verify that any person claiming to act on behalf of a juridical person is authorized to do so. Additionally, the identity of that authorized person should be verified.
- Legal Status Verification: Insurers should identify and verify the legal status of a juridical person through various supporting documents. This includes details such as the name, legal form, proof of existence, powers that regulate and bind the entity, address of the registered office/main place of business, and details of authorized individuals acting on behalf of the client.
- Ascertaining Beneficial Owner(s): Insurers must ascertain the beneficial owner(s) of the juridical person, ensuring transparency and understanding of ultimate ownership and control.
- It is important to note that insurance companies are prohibited from allowing the opening or maintenance of

accounts that are anonymous, under fictitious names, or on behalf of individuals whose identity has not been disclosed or verified.

KYC IN E-COMMERCE

KYC (Know Your Customer) in eCommerce refers to the process of verifying the identity of customers before allowing them to engage in transactions on an online platform or marketplace. It is a crucial step in establishing trust, mitigating risks, and complying with regulatory requirements in the digital commerce space.

Ecommerce companies verify the identities and information of the individuals or entities involved in their platform through KYC. Many of the eCommerce companies also offer their payment solutions like their own payment gateways like Amazon Pay or Alipay. These payment services fall under the payment banking services and the regulations applicable to the banks become applicable to these companies. Non-compliance of the KYC norms lead to regulatory penalties and fines. [vi]

The exact verification process may vary depending on the company and the specific requirements. Here are the primary parties that ecommerce companies typically verify through KYC:

1. Sellers/Merchants: Ecommerce platforms need to verify the identities and legitimacy of sellers or merchants who wish to list and sell products on their platform. This verification process ensures that only genuine businesses or individuals with valid credentials are allowed to operate on the platform. Sellers are typically required to provide

identification documents, business licenses, tax registrations, and other relevant information to establish their authenticity. In 2016, it was reported that counterfeit products were being sold by unauthorized third-party sellers on Amazon's platform. These sellers were able to evade proper verification measures, resulting in the sale of fake and low-quality goods to unsuspecting customers. This incident not only tarnished Amazon's reputation as a trusted marketplace but also raised concerns about the company's ability to ensure the authenticity and quality of products sold on its platform. It highlighted the importance of robust seller KYC procedures to prevent such reputational damage and protect customer trust.

2. Buyers/Customers: In some cases, ecommerce companies may also verify the identities of buyers or customers, especially when they offer services such as digital payments or have loyalty programs. By verifying the identities of customers, ecommerce companies can ensure the security of transactions, prevent fraudulent activities, and comply with legal and regulatory requirements.

3. Third-Party Service Providers: Ecommerce companies may engage with various third-party service providers, such as logistics partners or payment gateways, to facilitate the smooth operation of their platform. KYC may be conducted on these service providers to ensure they meet certain standards and comply with regulations. This helps ecommerce companies to maintain the integrity of their platform and protect the interests of their users.

In eCommerce, KYC involves collecting and verifying certain information about customers to confirm their identity and assess the level of risk associated with them. The specific requirements and procedures may vary depending on the country, platform, or regulatory framework. However, the general purpose is to ensure that customers are genuine, prevent fraudulent activities, protect against money laundering, and enhance the overall security of online transactions.

STEPS IN KYC PROCESS OF ECOMMERCE

The KYC process in eCommerce typically involves the following steps:

- Customer Information Collection: The platform collects basic details from the customer, such as name, address, contact information, and sometimes additional details like date of birth or identification numbers.

- Document Verification: Customers are usually required to provide supporting documents to validate their identity. These documents may include government-issued identification cards (e.g., driver's license, passport), proof of address (e.g., utility bills, bank statements), or any other relevant identification documents.

- Identity Verification: The collected documents and information are then verified to confirm the authenticity of the customer's identity. This can be done through various methods, including manual review by platform staff or automated identity verification services that analyze the provided documents and perform checks against databases or other reliable sources.

- Risk Assessment: Once the identity is verified, the platform may assess the level of risk associated with the customer. This assessment considers factors like the customer's transaction history, geographic location, purchase patterns, and any other relevant information. Based on the risk assessment, the platform may categorize customers into different risk levels, such as low-risk, medium-risk, or high-risk.

- Ongoing Monitoring: In some cases, eCommerce platforms may conduct periodic reviews or monitoring of customer accounts to detect any suspicious activities or changes in customer behavior that might indicate potential fraud or compliance risks.

CASE STUDIES ON ECOMMERCE KYC

Here are some case studies on the subject of KYC in eCommerce. These case studies demonstrate that KYC is a critical aspect of eCommerce platforms, enabling them to create secure and reliable environments for both buyers and sellers. By implementing effective KYC processes, eCommerce companies can prevent fraud, maintain regulatory compliance, build trust, and provide a safe and positive user experience.

1. Amazon: Amazon, one of the world's largest eCommerce companies, has implemented KYC measures to ensure a secure and trustworthy platform. They require sellers to provide various documents, such as business licenses, tax registrations, and identity proofs, to verify their identities and legitimacy. This helps in weeding out fraudulent sellers and maintaining a reputable marketplace.

2. Flipkart: Flipkart, a leading eCommerce platform in India, has implemented a robust KYC process for sellers. They require sellers to provide their PAN (Permanent Account Number) card, address proof, and bank account details for verification. This helps in preventing fake sellers and ensures that genuine sellers are registered on the platform.

3. Alibaba: Alibaba, the multinational conglomerate based in China, has incorporated KYC measures to enhance trust and security. They have implemented a system called "Alibaba TrustPass" which involves verifying the identity, business licenses, and contact information of sellers. This helps in building credibility and protecting buyers from potential scams or counterfeit products.

4. Paytm: Paytm, a popular digital payment and eCommerce platform in India, has implemented KYC for its users. They require customers to complete their KYC by providing identity and address proofs. This helps in complying with regulatory requirements and enables users to access advanced features such as higher transaction limits and wallet-to-bank transfers.

5. Shopify: Shopify, a leading eCommerce platform that enables businesses to set up their online stores, provides KYC tools and integrations for its merchants. By partnering with third-party KYC service providers, Shopify allows merchants to verify their identities and protect their businesses from fraudulent activities. This helps in building trust between merchants and customers.

KYC IN GAMING

Online casino KYC (Know Your Customer) procedures are a mandatory component of anti-money laundering legislation, subject to varying guidance from regulatory bodies in different jurisdictions. The overarching objective is to identify customers, accurately verify their information, and engage in ongoing monitoring of transactions and behavior.

The Financial Crimes Enforcement Network (FinCEN) provides guidance outlining essential procedures that online casinos should implement to maintain compliance with the Bank Secrecy Act (BSA). These procedures include independent compliance testing to assess money laundering risks associated with each product offered, as well as protocols for identifying and verifying customers using official documentation and personally identifiable information (PII). Additionally, online casinos are required to allocate resources to train staff on compliance matters and appoint specific individuals to ensure day-to-day adherence to regulations and the maintenance of records.

The American Gaming Association (AMA) has also issued its own guidance on best practices for anti-money laundering (AML) compliance and KYC procedures. The document emphasizes the significance of rigorous risk assessments, preventive measures, and customer due diligence, along with comprehensive employee training. While the guidance recommends consistent monitoring of suspicious transactions, it strongly advises the implementation of robust KYC procedures to securely verify user identities using documentation and personal details, with the involvement of third-party independent verifiers.

Similarly, European Union (EU) regulations stipulate that online gambling entities must prioritize the "identification of the customer and verification of the customer's identity based on documents, data, or information obtained from a reliable and independent source." UK regulatory bodies also require online casinos to make significant efforts to establish customer identities through additional documents, data, or information.

It is crucial to note that different jurisdictions may apply the KYC process at different stages, as per strict risk assessment regulations imposed on online casinos. For instance, EU casinos are not required to trigger KYC checks until customers deposit over 2000 EUR. However, it is important to understand that users who are citizens of the US and UK must undergo KYC checks when opening accounts.

The customary procedure for verifying a customer's identity involves the submission of personal information and supporting official documentation. Online gambling platforms then transmit this documentation to independent third-party verifiers who authenticate its validity and compare the information against global databases. Through this process, third-party verifiers can confirm the true identities of customers.

Furthermore, by cross-referencing customer data with global watchlists, verifiers identify Politically Exposed Persons (PEPs), individuals holding positions of political power who are susceptible to corruption. These checks also flag any financial sanctions imposed on users, which may pose a risk to the casino.

In accordance with recent regulatory enhancements, third-party verifiers must also compare customer data with self-exclusion lists to prevent access to casinos by individuals who have voluntarily excluded themselves due to gambling addiction.

Lastly, these checks may require users to disclose their sources of income to identify any suspicious transactions.

CHALLENGES OF ID VERIFICATION FOR CASINOS

Manual identity verification and KYC procedures in the online gambling industry suffer from drawbacks such as being slow, expensive, and cumbersome. The lack of standardization regarding required documentation leads to a poor user experience, as different establishments have varying requirements, resulting in users repeatedly submitting their data. This not only poses a security risk as users provide sensitive information to multiple gambling organizations but also leads to user dropouts and a shift towards less reputable sites that do not require verification. The increasing demand for online gambling services results in a significant backlog of KYC applications, causing delays of over a week for some KYC approvals.

The increasing cost of compliance is another significant challenge. With online casinos now classified as non-bank financial institutions, stricter compliance rules are in place. Consequently, gambling entities must allocate resources to hire expensive fraud management teams, compliance officers, and Money Laundering Reporting Officers (MLROs) to ensure the implementation and adherence to KYC and AML procedures.

The disclosure of sensitive data to numerous third-party verifiers exposes this information to potential misuse by malicious actors. As third-party verifiers are human, they are susceptible to being deceived by fake documents and fraudulent information, further compromising the accuracy and reliability of identity verification processes.

The cross-border nature of online gambling introduces additional challenges, as players come from various countries.

Verification of players from smaller countries may pose difficulties for operators who lack the necessary tools to authenticate identification documents accurately. Consequently, high-risk users may go undetected.

The lack of standardization among regulatory bodies creates uncertainty for online casinos striving to maintain compliance. For example, EU-based casinos face difficulties determining when to conduct KYC checks, as EU legislation suggests verification should occur when a player deposits over 2000 EUR, whereas stricter UK legislation recommends verifying identities upon account opening. This inconsistency adds to the confusion faced by online gambling entities, given the significant fines associated with non-compliance.

These challenges highlight the inadequacy of manual KYC processing for online gambling establishments, as it lacks scalability. As user enrolment on online gambling sites increases, the cost and time required for ID verification procedures also escalate. To address these issues and ensure compliance with regulations while maintaining efficiency and cost-effectiveness, alternative solutions for KYC and identity verification are necessary for online casinos now and in the future.

KYC IN REAL ESTATE

Knowing the customer is important for real estate companies in India for several reasons. Firstly, it helps verify the identity and background of the customers, ensuring they are genuine and trustworthy individuals. This is crucial in a high-value transaction like real estate, where fraud and scams can occur. Secondly, customer information enables real estate companies to assess the financial capabilities of customers, ensuring they have the necessary funds to complete the transaction. It also helps in complying with anti-money laundering (AML) regulations and preventing illicit activities.

REGULATIONS GOVERNING REAL ESTATE

According to the PMLA, real estate agents, developers, and any other person carrying out real estate transactions of a certain threshold value are categorized as "reporting entities" and are required to comply with the reporting obligations set forth by the FIU. These reporting entities need to maintain records of transactions, conduct customer due diligence, and report any suspicious transactions or activities to the FIU within the specified timelines and in the prescribed format.

The real estate sector is regulated by several authorities and has specific regulations pertaining to Know Your Customer (KYC) requirements. Here are some key regulations for KYC in real estate in India:

- The Real Estate (Regulation and Development) Act, 2016 (RERA): RERA is a central legislation that aims to regulate the real estate sector in India. Under RERA, developers and real estate agents are required to maintain records of their customers and perform KYC verification. They need to collect and verify documents such as identity proof, address proof, and PAN (Permanent Account Number) for transactions above a specified threshold.
- Prevention of Money Laundering Act, 2002 (PMLA): PMLA is a legislation enacted to prevent money laundering and combat the financing of terrorism.

Real estate developers and brokers are classified as 'obligated entities' under PMLA, requiring them to comply with KYC norms. They need to conduct customer due diligence, maintain records of transactions, and report suspicious transactions to the appropriate authorities.
- Aadhaar (Targeted Delivery of Financial and Other Subsidies, Benefits and Services) Act, 2016: Aadhaar is a unique identification number issued by the Unique Identification Authority of India (UIDAI). While it is not specifically a KYC regulation for real estate, the use of Aadhaar may be required for identity verification and authentication purposes during real estate transactions.
- Goods and Services Tax (GST) regulations: GST is an indirect tax applicable to the sale of goods and services in India. Real estate transactions are subject to GST, and compliance with GST regulations may involve the collection and verification of customer details for invoicing and taxation purposes.

EXAMPLES OF KYC REQUIREMENTS IN REAL ESTATE

Property Registration: During the registration of a property, buyers and sellers are required to provide KYC documents, such as identification proof (e.g., Aadhaar card, PAN card, passport), address proof, and photographs. These documents are submitted to the concerned authorities for verification and record-keeping purposes.

- Home Loan Applications: When individuals apply for home loans from banks or financial institutions to finance their property purchase, KYC documentation

is necessary. This includes providing identity proof, address proof, income proof, and other supporting documents as required by the lending institution. KYC helps lenders assess the credibility of the borrowers and mitigate the risk of fraudulent loan applications.
- Tenant Verification: Landlords often conduct KYC checks on prospective tenants before renting out their properties. This involves verifying the identity, address, employment details, and background information of the tenants to ensure their reliability and security. KYC helps landlords make informed decisions and safeguard their property interests.
- Builder-Buyer Agreements: Real estate developers or builders may perform KYC on potential buyers before entering into agreements. This includes collecting and verifying KYC documents to establish the identity and credibility of the buyers. KYC helps builders ensure transparency, prevent fraudulent transactions, and maintain proper records of their customers.
- Compliance with Anti-Money Laundering (AML) Regulations: Real estate transactions, especially high-value ones, are subject to AML regulations. KYC plays a crucial role in fulfilling AML requirements by verifying the identities of buyers, sellers, and other parties involved in the transaction. This helps in preventing money laundering, terrorist financing, and other illicit activities in the real estate sector.

Knowing the customer allows real estate companies to personalize their services, understand customer preferences, and provide a better overall experience.

Real estate transactions can involve large amounts of money, making it vulnerable to money laundering activities. KYC helps identify the source of funds and ensures transparency in transactions, reducing the risk of illegal activities.

Secondly, India has been grappling with the issue of black money in the real estate sector. KYC helps track the flow of funds, discouraging cash transactions and promoting legitimate financial practices. It aids in curbing the circulation of unaccounted money in the real estate market.

By implementing KYC, the real estate sector can enhance transparency and accountability. It creates a standardized process for documenting and verifying customer information, making it easier to trace property ownership and maintain a reliable database of property transactions.

Effective KYC measures in real estate also instill confidence in investors and stakeholders. It demonstrates a commitment to maintaining ethical practices and reduces the risk of fraudulent activities, attracting genuine investors and fostering a healthy and trustworthy real estate market.

KYC ON-BOARDING PROGRAM

A KYC (Know Your Customer) onboarding program refers to the process and set of activities undertaken by businesses or financial institutions to verify and authenticate the identity of their customers during the account opening or client onboarding stage. The primary goal of a KYC onboarding program is to ensure compliance with regulatory requirements, prevent fraud, and assess the risk associated with potential customers.

The elements of a KYC onboarding program typically include:

CUSTOMER IDENTIFICATION

This involves collecting relevant information from customers to establish their identity, such as name, address, date of birth, and identification documents like passports or driver's licenses. It also includes gathering additional information for enhanced due diligence, such as the purpose of the account and the nature of the customer's business activities.

While it is sufficient to collect customer information during the account opening process, financial institutions are required to verify the account holder's identity within a reasonable timeframe.

This verification process involves various procedures, which may include the examination of documents provided by the customer, as well as non-documentary methods. Non-documentary methods may involve cross-referencing the information provided by the customer with consumer reporting agencies, public databases, and other due diligence measures. In some cases, a combination of both document-based and non-documentary methods may be used.

These verification procedures are fundamental to the Customer Identification Program (CIP) and are part of the broader Anti-Money Laundering (AML) compliance requirements. It is important that these policies are not implemented haphazardly, but rather they should be clearly defined and documented to provide ongoing guidance to staff, executives, and regulators.

The specific policies adopted by financial institutions will depend on their risk-based approach, taking into consideration factors such as the

- types of accounts offered,
- the methods used for account opening,
- the availability of identifying information,
- the size and location of the institution,
- Characteristics of the customer base.

Additionally, the policies may vary based on the types of products and services utilized by customers in different geographic locations.

Verifying the authenticity of customer-provided identification documents is a crucial element of KYC onboarding. This can involve using technologies like facial recognition, document scanning, or biometric authentication to validate the identity

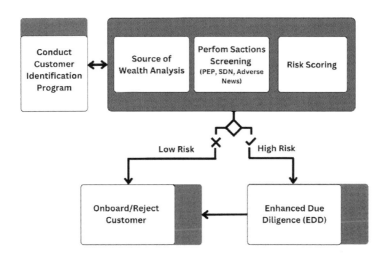

of the customer and ensure that the provided documents are not forged or manipulated.

The CIP is a critical step in KYC compliance as it helps financial institutions establish the true identity of their customers and ensure they are not involved in illegal activities. By implementing robust CIP procedures, institutions can strengthen their risk management practices and adhere to regulatory requirements.

CUSTOMER DUE DILIGENCE (CDD)

Once the customer identification is done it is necessary to perform the customer due diligence. CDD involves assessing the risk profile of customers to determine the level of due diligence required. This step includes evaluating factors such as the customer's source of funds, business relationships, and any potential exposure to higher-risk activities or jurisdictions. There are three known types of due diligence in Indian Banks and Financial institutions.

1. Simplified Due Diligence (SDD) refers to situations where the risk of money laundering or terrorist funding is considered to be low, and therefore, a full Customer Due Diligence (CDD) process is not necessary. SDD is typically applied to accounts or customers with low value or low-risk profiles. In these cases, a simplified set of information and verification procedures are employed to meet the regulatory requirements.
2. Basic Customer Due Diligence (CDD) involves gathering information from all customers to verify their identity and assess the risks associated with them. It is a fundamental step in the due diligence process that ensures the institution has a clear understanding of the customer's identity and potential risks involved in their activities. The information collected during CDD helps in establishing the customer's identity, understanding their business relationships, and assessing any suspicious or unusual transactions.
3. Enhanced Due Diligence (EDD) goes beyond the basic information gathered in CDD and involves collecting additional information for customers deemed to be higher-risk. EDD provides a more comprehensive understanding of the customer's activities, business associations, and potential risk factors. The purpose of

EDD is to obtain a deeper insight into the customer's profile and behavior, enabling the institution to mitigate any associated risks effectively. While certain factors for conducting EDD may be prescribed by country-specific legislations, financial institutions have the responsibility to assess their own risks and implement appropriate measures to ensure that their customers are not involved in illicit activities.

Simplified Due Diligence is used in low-risk situations where a full Customer Due Diligence is not required. The Customer Due Diligence is the basic information gathering process for all customers, and Enhanced Due Diligence is an additional level of due diligence applied to higher-risk customers to obtain a more detailed understanding of their activities and mitigate associated risks. The specific requirements and measures for conducting EDD may vary depending on the country's regulations, but financial institutions have the autonomy to determine and implement their own risk management practices to ensure the integrity of their customer base.

SOURCE OF FUNDS/WEALTH

Evaluating the source of a customer's funds or wealth is important to ensure they are legitimate and derived from legal activities. This may involve requesting documentation or conducting interviews to understand the origin of the funds. The purpose of the source of funds/wealth assessment is to ensure that the customer's financial resources come from legitimate sources and are not associated with illegal activities such as money laundering or terrorist financing. Financial institutions have a responsibility to prevent the use of their services for illicit purposes, and understanding the source of funds/wealth is a critical component of risk management and compliance.

During the assessment, the financial institution may request documentation or supporting evidence from the customer to substantiate the origin of their funds or wealth. This may include:

- Bank Statements: The customer may be asked to provide recent bank statements that show the history of their transactions and the inflow of funds into their accounts.
- Tax Returns: Individuals may be required to provide their personal or business tax returns to demonstrate their income and financial activities.
- Business Records: For customers involved in business activities, financial institutions may request business records, such as financial statements, invoices, contracts, or proof of ownership, to verify the legitimacy of their funds.
- Investment Statements: Customers who derive their wealth from investments may need to provide investment account statements or documentation related to their investment activities.
- Inheritance or Gift Documentation: In cases where funds or wealth are inherited or received as a gift, the financial institution may ask for legal documentation, such as inheritance certificates or gift deeds, to validate the source.

POLITICALLY EXPOSED PERSONS (PEP) SCREENING

In the realm of comprehensive customer due diligence (CDD), one crucial step is to conduct screening of customers against Politically Exposed Person (PEP) lists. This step holds great significance as it helps in the identification of individuals who currently hold or have previously held significant public positions. Such individuals are deemed to have a higher risk profile due to their potential involvement in corruption, bribery, or money laundering activities.

In the specific context of India, Riskpro offers a highly comprehensive solution for screening Indian politicians. Given the diverse political landscape and the prominence of politicians in the country, it becomes imperative for financial institutions and organizations to have a robust mechanism in place to identify any potential risks associated with these individuals.

Riskpro's solution is designed to cater specifically to the Indian market, ensuring an extensive and effective screening process for politicians. By leveraging Riskpro's solution, organizations operating in India can enhance their KYC and AML procedures and mitigate the risks associated with politically exposed individuals.[vii]

It is important to note that screening customers against PEP lists is not limited to India alone. It is a globally recognized practice that forms an integral part of KYC and AML compliance efforts worldwide. Financial institutions and organizations across different jurisdictions deploy similar solutions to screen individuals holding prominent public positions and safeguard themselves against potential risks associated with money laundering and corruption.

Financial institutions (referred to as REs) have the option to establish a relationship with PEPs in India under certain conditions:

- Sufficient information about the PEP's background, including the sources of their funds and accounts of their family members and close relatives, should be gathered.
- The identity of the PEP must be verified before accepting them as a customer.
- The decision to open an account for a PEP should be made at a senior level in accordance with the REs' Customer Acceptance Policy.
- All accounts of PEPs should be subjected to enhanced monitoring on an ongoing basis to detect any suspicious activities.
- If an existing customer or the beneficial owner of an existing account becomes a PEP, senior management's approval should be obtained to continue the business relationship.
- The Customer Due Diligence (CDD) measures applicable to PEPs, including enhanced monitoring, should be followed.

When a PEP is the beneficial owner, meaning if the PEP has control over the account without necessarily being the account holder, even then the Reporting entities follow the same procedures.

SANCTIONS AND WATCHLIST SCREENING

In the context of Know Your Customer (KYC) procedures, conducting checks against global sanctions lists, terrorist watchlists, and other relevant databases is a crucial step in identifying any potential association between customers and individuals, entities, or countries involved in illegal activities.

These checks involve comparing the information provided by customers against comprehensive databases that contain information on individuals or entities that are subject to sanctions or are known to have links with terrorism or illicit activities. The purpose of these checks is to identify any matches or similarities between customer information and the records in these databases.

By checking customers against these lists and databases, financial institutions and other entities can enhance their ability to detect and prevent transactions or relationships that may pose a risk of involvement in illegal activities such as money laundering, terrorist financing, or other forms of financial crime.

The lists and databases used for these checks are typically compiled and maintained by international organizations, regulatory bodies, law enforcement agencies, and government entities. They contain information on individuals, organizations, and countries that have been designated as high-risk or subject to sanctions due to their involvement in illicit activities, violations of international laws, or connections to terrorism.

The purpose of these checks is to ensure compliance with regulatory requirements and to safeguard the integrity of the financial system by preventing illicit funds from entering the system or being used for illegal purposes. By identifying any association between customers and sanctioned individuals or entities, financial institutions can take appropriate actions, such as reporting the suspicious activity, freezing assets, or refusing to establish business relationships with high-risk individuals or entities.

The checking process typically involves automated screening mechanisms that compare customer data, such as names, addresses, identification numbers, and other relevant information, against the lists and databases. If a potential match or similarity is identified, further investigation or enhanced due diligence measures may be undertaken to determine the nature and extent of the association.

Overall, checking customers against global sanctions lists, terrorist watchlists, and relevant databases serves as an important risk mitigation measure in the KYC process, helping to identify and mitigate potential risks associated with customers who may have connections to illegal activities or pose a threat to the integrity of the financial system.

ADVERSE MEDIA CHECKS

Adverse media screening is a component of the Know Your Customer (KYC) process that involves reviewing and analyzing public information sources to identify any negative or adverse news, reports, or media coverage related to individuals or entities. It is an essential step in assessing the potential risks associated with a customer and ensuring compliance with anti-money laundering (AML) and counter-terrorism financing (CTF) regulations.

During adverse media screening, various sources of information are scanned, including news articles, online publications, regulatory announcements, government databases, court records, and other publicly available sources. The purpose is to uncover any information that could indicate involvement in illegal activities, financial crimes, corruption, fraud, or reputational risks.

The screening process involves using specialized software or tools that employ natural language processing (NLP) and data mining techniques to analyze and extract relevant information from vast amounts of unstructured data. The extracted data is then matched against predefined keywords, phrases, or risk indicators to identify potential matches or red flags.

Adverse media screening helps financial institutions and other organizations to identify customers who may have connections to high-risk individuals, politically exposed persons (PEPs), sanctioned entities, or criminal networks. It allows them to assess the reputation and integrity of customers, detect potential conflicts of interest, and make informed decisions regarding the establishment or continuation of business relationships.

By conducting thorough adverse media screening, organizations can enhance their due diligence efforts, mitigate the risks associated with money laundering, terrorist financing, fraud, and other illicit activities, and demonstrate compliance with regulatory requirements. If any adverse information is identified during the screening process, further investigation or enhanced due diligence measures may be undertaken to determine the significance of the findings and the potential impact on the risk profile of the customer.

It is important to note that adverse media screening is not a standalone process but rather an integral part of the broader KYC framework. It complements other KYC procedures such as identity verification, risk assessment, ongoing monitoring, and customer due diligence, providing valuable insights into the background and behavior of customers.

RISK SCORING

Customer risk rating, also known as customer risk profiling or customer risk assessment, is a process used by financial institutions and other organizations to evaluate the level of risk associated with a particular customer. It involves assigning a risk rating or score to customers based on various factors, including channel, geography, product, transaction, customer characteristics, and external risk indicators.

The customer risk rating is determined by analyzing and assessing both internal and external factors that can contribute to the risk profile of a customer. Let's explore the different elements that contribute to the customer risk rating:

- Channel Risk: This refers to the risk associated with the specific channels or delivery channels through which the customer conducts transactions. Different channels may have varying levels of risk. For example, online transactions may be considered higher risk due to the potential for cyber threats or identity theft.
- Geography Risk: The geographic location of the customer and the jurisdictions in which they operate can impact the risk rating. Some regions or countries may have higher risks associated with money

laundering, terrorism financing, or corruption, while others may have stronger regulatory frameworks.
- Product Risk: The type of product or service utilized by the customer can influence the risk rating. Certain products or services, such as international wire transfers or high-value investments, may present higher risks for financial crimes.
- Transaction Risk: The nature and volume of transactions conducted by the customer are evaluated for potential risk. Unusual or suspicious transaction patterns, large cash transactions, or frequent transfers to high-risk jurisdictions may increase the customer's risk rating.
- Customer Risk: Factors related to the customer's profile and behavior are taken into consideration. This includes assessing the customer's background, occupation, source of funds, politically exposed person (PEP) status, and any previous involvement in financial crimes.
- External Risk Indicators: External risk factors, such as sanctions lists, terrorist watchlists, adverse media coverage, or other public information, are analyzed to identify any associations or red flags that may elevate the customer's risk rating.

By considering these multiple dimensions, financial institutions can develop a comprehensive understanding of the risk posed by a customer. The risk rating helps in determining the level of due diligence and monitoring required for that customer. Higher-risk customers may undergo enhanced due diligence procedures, such as additional documentation, verification, or ongoing monitoring.

The specific methodology and criteria for customer risk rating can vary between organizations and may be influenced by regulatory requirements and industry best practices. The risk rating is typically assigned through a systematic and consistent approach, ensuring that customers are categorized and treated appropriately based on their risk levels.

ONGOING MONITORING

KYC onboarding is not a one-time process. Financial institutions are responsible for continuously monitoring customer accounts for suspicious activities or changes in risk profile. This may involve transaction monitoring, reviewing customer data periodically, and updating customer information as necessary.

In order to ensure effective risk mitigation, it is insufficient to conduct customer checks only at the initial stage. It is essential to implement an ongoing monitoring program to continuously assess and oversee customer activity. This entails monitoring financial transactions and accounts based on predetermined thresholds that are established as part of the customer's risk profile.

Depending on the specific customer and the risk mitigation strategy in place, there are other factors that should be monitored.

These may include

- identifying sudden spikes in activity,
- unusual cross-border transactions,
- presence of individuals on sanction lists,
- Any adverse media mentions related to the customer.

If any account activity is considered unusual, there might be a requirement to file a Suspicious Activity Report (SAR) to the appropriate authorities.

Conducting periodic reviews of the account and associated risks is also considered a best practice. This involves ensuring that the account record is up-to-date, assessing whether the type and number of transactions align with the stated purpose of the account, and evaluating whether the assigned risk level corresponds appropriately with the nature and volume of transactions.

In general, the level of transaction monitoring is determined based on a risk-based assessment. This means that the extent and intensity of monitoring activities depend on the perceived level of risk associated with the customer and their transactions.

Under the RBI guidelines, banks and financial institutions are required to implement robust systems and processes for ongoing monitoring of customer accounts. This includes the following key aspects:

Transaction Monitoring

Banks should have systems in place to monitor customer transactions on a regular basis. This involves setting thresholds and parameters to identify transactions that deviate from the customer's normal behavior or fall within suspicious patterns. Unusual or high-value transactions should be subject to additional scrutiny and investigation.

Risk-based Approach

The level and intensity of ongoing monitoring should be commensurate with the risk profile of the customer. Higher-risk customers, such as politically exposed persons (PEPs) or those engaged in high-value transactions, should receive enhanced monitoring compared to lower-risk customers.

Periodic Account Reviews: Banks are required to conduct periodic reviews of customer accounts to ensure that the information and documentation on record are up-to-date and accurate. This includes verifying the customer's identity, assessing the ongoing risk associated with the customer, and validating the purpose and nature of the customer's transactions.

Record-keeping: Adequate records of customer transactions, identification documents, and ongoing monitoring activities should be maintained by the bank as part of their compliance obligations. These records should be easily accessible for internal and regulatory audits.

Reporting of Suspicious Transactions: If any suspicious or unusual activity is detected during the ongoing monitoring process, banks are obligated to file a Suspicious Transaction Report (STR) with the Financial Intelligence Unit (FIU) of India.

The RBI guidelines emphasize the importance of continuous monitoring and diligent oversight to mitigate the risks of money laundering, terrorist financing, and other financial crimes. Banks are expected to establish effective systems, employ trained staff, and leverage technology to facilitate ongoing monitoring and ensure compliance with KYC requirements.

KYC COMPLIANCE AND REGULATORY FRAMEWORK

The KYC norms in India are an important aspect of the country's anti-money laundering and anti-terrorism financing measures. These norms are designed to meet the requirements of the Financial Action Task Force (FATF), an inter-governmental organization that aims to prevent the misuse of the financial system for illegal activities such as money laundering, terrorist financing, and weapons proliferation.

The FATF issues recommendations that lay down standards for its member countries to adopt. Although these recommendations are not legally binding, failure to comply with them can have serious consequences on a member state's economic interests. As a result, domestic legislation in many countries, including India, is shaped by these recommendations.

One of the key FATF recommendations is that reporting entities, such as financial institutions and designated nonfinancial businesses, should carry out appropriate customer identification and verification procedures. This is aimed at promoting greater transparency and accountability in the formal financial system.

PREVENTION OF MONEY LAUNDERING ACT (PMLA)

In India, customer identification requirements have been implemented on various financial entities under the Prevention of Money Laundering Act, 2002 ("PMLA") and rules issued thereunder, even before India became a member of the FATF in 2010. Sectoral regulators such as the Reserve Bank of India (RBI), Securities and Exchange Board of India (SEBI), Insurance Regulatory Development Authority of India (IRDAI), and the Pension Fund Regulatory and Development Authority (PFRDA) also specify specific obligations in this regard.

The PMLA (Prevention of Money Laundering Act) and PML (Prevention of Money Laundering) Rules impose three significant obligations on Financial Institutions (FIs) concerning Customer Due Diligence (CDD).

Firstly, FIs, such as banks, are required to identify their customers, verify their identity, and collect information on the purpose and intended nature of the business relationship. They must also determine if the customer is acting on behalf of a beneficial owner and, if so, verify the identity of such an entity. This is to ensure that the FI knows the actual person they are dealing with and the source of their funds. Additionally, the PMLA and PML Rules prohibit anonymous accounts or accounts in fictitious names to prevent money laundering or terrorist financing.

Secondly, within give time frame of the commencement of an account-based relationship, every FI must file an electronic copy of the customer's KYC (Know Your Customer) records with the centralised Central KYC Record Registry (CKYCR Registry).

This helps prevent the duplication of KYC documents for the same customer across multiple FIs, and customers are issued a unique KYC identifier which can be used to carry out KYC across FIs.

Thirdly, every FI must exercise ongoing due diligence with respect to the business relationship with every customer and closely examine each transaction to ensure consistency with the customer's business and risk profile, "and where necessary, the source of funds." The level of due diligence required may vary based on the risk profile of the customer, ranging from simplified CDD to EDD (Enhanced Due Diligence) depending on the customer's risk profile or the FI's suspicions of a deviance between what is known of the customer and the activities being carried out. This helps the FIs to identify any suspicious transactions or activities and report them to the relevant authorities promptly.

PML Rules have stringent requirements for FIs to comply with to prevent money laundering and terrorist financing. FIs must identify their customers, verify their identity, determine if they are acting on behalf of a beneficial owner, and exercise ongoing due diligence to monitor their business relationship and transactions closely.

ENHANCED DUE DILIGENCE

Enhanced Due Diligence (EDD) refers to an additional level of scrutiny that Financial Institutions (FIs) need to perform while onboarding customers, especially for high-risk customers. The requirement of EDD in India is governed by the Prevention of Money Laundering Act (PMLA), and the FIs must conduct EDD before the commencement of each "specified transaction." In case a specified transaction is suspicious or likely to involve proceeds of crime, the FI must increase its monitoring of the business relationship and scrutinize transactions more closely.

PEPs, non-face-to-face customers, and correspondent banking relationships are examples of accounts that require EDD. Banks can apply EDD measures based on a risk assessment for higher risk customers whose sources of funds are unclear, taking into consideration the type of customer, business relationship, and nature and value of transactions based on the overall money laundering/terrorist financing (ML/TF) risk involved.

The responsibility of conducting EDD ultimately lies with the FIs, and they have considerable discretion in determining when to conduct EDD, which proposed transactions necessitate authentication, and what additional information to seek while balancing AML/CFT and privacy measures. However, since the FATF framework does not require countries to consider the privacy costs of conducting EDD, privacy concerns have not been baked into the design and architecture of Indian law.

Therefore, FIs need to exercise discretion while keeping in mind the privacy implications and the unintended consequences of conducting EDD. Banks may collect sensitive personal data as part of their EDD procedures without notice to their customers and without their consent, which raises privacy concerns. Although the RBI requires banks to collect only relevant information, the level of regulatory oversight over banks' data processing activities is unclear. Increased regulatory pressure on FIs to do EDD has driven de-banking in the money transfer organizations.

The lack of specific guidance leaves the EDD process open-ended and at the discretion of banks. The Reserve Bank of India (RBI) has laid down guidelines for gathering "sufficient information" on Politically Exposed Persons (PEPs) intending to establish a relationship with the bank. Banks are required to verify the identity of the PEP, seek information about their sources of funds, and subject their account to "enhanced monitoring on an ongoing basis." Similar processes have been mandated by SEBI and IRDA for Mutual Funds/registered intermediaries before establishing relationships with PEPs.

ONGOING DUE DILIGENCE AND TRANSACTION MONITORING

Another important provision of The PMLA is the Ongoing Due Diligence and Transaction Monitoring. It requires banks and other financial institutions to establish and maintain policies and procedures for identifying and monitoring suspicious transactions. The Reserve Bank of India (RBI) has also issued guidelines and directives to banks and other financial institutions for implementing effective anti-money laundering measures, including ongoing due diligence and transaction monitoring.

Ongoing due diligence (ODD) refers to the continuous monitoring of customer accounts and transactions to ensure that the FI has up-to-date information about the customer's identity, business activities, and risk profile. This includes reviewing and updating customer information, assessing any changes in the customer's risk profile, and conducting enhanced due diligence (EDD) on high-risk customers.

Transaction monitoring (TM) involves the ongoing monitoring of customer transactions to detect any unusual or suspicious activities. FIs use a variety of tools and techniques to monitor transactions, including automated systems, alert mechanisms, and manual review processes. The goal is to identify potential instances of money laundering, terrorism financing, or other illicit activities, and report them to the relevant authorities.

Instances of Increased Monitoring

Clause 36 of the RBI Master Direction on KYC outlines the instances where financial institutions (FIs) are required to apply increased monitoring on certain transactions. These instances are as follows:

- Large and complex transactions with unusual/inconsistent patterns: FIs should monitor transactions that are unusually large or complex and exhibit patterns that are inconsistent with a customer's typical transaction history.
- Transactions that have no apparent economic rationale or legitimate purpose: FIs should be cautious of transactions that have no apparent legitimate

economic purpose or appear to be structured in a way to evade regulatory scrutiny.

- Transactions exceeding the prescribed thresholds for specific categories of accounts: FIs should monitor transactions that exceed the prescribed thresholds for specific types of accounts, such as high-value accounts or accounts held by politically exposed persons (PEPs).
- High account turnovers, inconsistent with the size of the balance maintained: FIs should monitor accounts that have high turnovers that are not consistent with the size of the balance maintained in the account.
- Deposit of third-party cheques, drafts, etc. in existing and newly opened accounts followed by cash withdrawals for large amounts: FIs should be cautious of customers who deposit third-party cheques, drafts, or other financial instruments into their accounts and then quickly withdraw large amounts of cash.

Increased monitoring of transactions is necessary to detect and prevent money laundering and terrorist financing activities. FIs should establish policies and procedures to detect suspicious transactions and report them to the relevant authorities as required by law.

ROLE OF RBI IN KYC COMPLIANCE

The primary objective of the KYC guidelines is to prevent banks from being exploited by criminal elements for money laundering activities, while also allowing banks to understand their customers and their financial transactions to manage risks effectively. Banks must develop their KYC policies that include four essential elements:

KYC COMPLIANCE AND REGULATORY FRAMEWORK

- Customer Acceptance Policy (CAP);
- Customer Identification Procedures;
- Transaction Monitoring; and
- Risk Management.

RBI circular RBI/DBR/2015-16/18, also known as Master Direction DBR.AML.BC.No.81/14.01.001/2015-16, is a comprehensive guideline issued by the Reserve Bank of India (RBI) regarding anti-money laundering (AML) measures for banks. The circular aims to ensure that banks have robust systems and controls in place to prevent money laundering and terrorist financing activities[viii].

For the purpose of KYC policy, a 'customer' is defined as a person or entity maintaining an account or business relationship with the bank, including beneficial owners, professional intermediary beneficiaries, and any individual or entity involved in a financial transaction that may pose a significant reputational or other risk to the bank.

CUSTOMER ACCEPTANCE POLICY (CAP)

Chapter 3 of the Master Direction deals with the Customer Acceptance Policy. Banks must develop a clear Customer Acceptance Policy that lays down explicit criteria for accepting customers. The policy must ensure that guidelines are in place concerning:

- No account should be opened in Benami or fictitious names.
- Clear parameters of risk perception must be defined to enable categorization of customers into low, medium, and high-risk categories, with the appropriate level of monitoring required for each.

- Documentation requirements and other information must be collected in respect of different categories of customers depending on perceived risk and in line with the requirements of the Prevention of Money Laundering Act, 2002, and guidelines issued by the Reserve Bank of India from time to time.
- Accounts should not be opened or maintained where appropriate customer due diligence measures cannot be applied due to non-cooperation or non-reliability of data/information furnished to the bank.
- Clear guidelines must be in place for when a customer is permitted to act on behalf of another person/entity, in conformity with established law and practice of banking.
- Necessary checks must be undertaken before opening a new account to ensure that the customer's identity does not match any person with a known criminal background or with banned entities such as individual terrorists or terrorist organizations.

Amendments in 2023

According to the amendments made to the Prevention of Money Laundering Act (PMLA) in 2023, the RBI's master directions were revised to incorporate these changes. According to the PMLA Amendments in 2023, the RBI master directions were changed to accommodate the amendments. One of the important changes is that when a reporting entity (RE) forms a suspicion of money laundering or terrorist financing and reasonably believes that conducting the customer due diligence (CDD) process will alert the customer, the RE shall refrain from pursuing the CDD process. Instead, it is required to file a suspicious transaction report (STR) with FIU-IND.

RISK MANAGEMENT

In Chapter IV of the Master Directions, it is stated that reporting entities (REs) should adopt a risk-based approach for risk management. This includes categorizing customers into low, medium, and high-risk categories based on their assessment and risk perception. REs are advised to establish broad principles for customer risk categorization.

The risk categorization should consider various parameters such as customer's identity, social/financial status, nature of business activity, information about the customer's business and location, geographical risks, types of products/services offered, delivery channels used, and types of transactions conducted. The ability to verify identity documents through online or other services offered by issuing authorities may also be taken into account.

The specific reasons for categorizing a customer and the categorization itself should be kept confidential to prevent tipping off the customer. However, non-intrusive information collected from different customer categories regarding perceived risk should be specified in the KYC policy.

The risk assessment can also consider relevant information from sources such as FATF Public Statement, reports, and guidance notes on KYC/AML issued by the Indian Banks Association (IBA), and other agencies.

CUSTOMER IDENTIFICATION

Chapter V of the RBI Master Directions outlines the Customer Identification Procedure (CIP) that reporting entities (REs) must follow. The key points covered in this chapter are as follows:

1. REs are required to identify customers in the following situations:
   - When establishing an account-based relationship with the customer.
   - When conducting international money transfer operations for non-account holders.
   - When there are doubts about the authenticity or adequacy of customer identification data.
   - When selling third-party products, making credit card payments, or conducting transactions exceeding INR 50,000.
   - When conducting transactions for walk-in customers exceeding INR 50,000, either as a single transaction or connected transactions.
   - When there is a suspicion that a customer is intentionally structuring transactions below the INR 50,000 threshold.
2. REs are not required to seek an introduction while opening accounts.
3. REs may rely on customer due diligence conducted by a third party for verifying customer identity during the

establishment of an account-based relationship. However, certain conditions must be met:

- The RE must obtain records or information of the customer due diligence from the third party within two days.
- The RE must ensure that identification data and relevant documentation will be made available by the third party upon request.
- The third party must be regulated, supervised, or monitored for compliance with customer due diligence and record-keeping requirements.
- The third party should not be based in a high-risk country or jurisdiction.

4. The ultimate responsibility for customer due diligence and enhanced due diligence measures lies with the RE.

CUSTOMER DUE DILIGENCE

Chapter VI of the Master Directions discuss the Customer Due Diligence (CDD) procedure, specifically focusing on individuals. The following points are highlighted:

- REs (Reporting Entities) need to obtain certain documents from individuals when establishing an account-based relationship or dealing with individuals who are beneficial owners, authorized signatories, or power of attorney holders related to any legal entity.

- The documents required include Aadhaar number, Permanent Account Number (PAN), proof of possession of Aadhaar number, KYC Identifier, and other documents related to the nature of business and financial status of the customer.
- Different provisions apply based on whether the customer submits Aadhaar number, proof of possession of Aadhaar, equivalent e-document of any Officially Valid Document (OVD), or KYC Identifier.
- Accounts opened using Aadhaar OTP based e-KYC in a non-face-to-face mode are subject to certain conditions, including specific consent from the customer for authentication through OTP, limitations on aggregate balance and credits, and restrictions on the duration of the account.
- REs may undertake Video-based Customer Identification Process (V-CIP) for new customer onboarding, conversion of existing accounts opened through Aadhaar OTP based e-KYC, and periodic updation of KYC.
- REs opting for V-CIP must adhere to minimum standards related to V-CIP infrastructure, procedures, and records/data management.
- The V-CIP infrastructure should comply with RBI guidelines on cybersecurity, ensure end-to-end

encryption, have face liveness/spoof detection technology, and undergo necessary tests and audits.
- The V-CIP procedure should involve trained officials, address disruptions, vary the sequence of questions, and capture audio-video recordings and identification information.

Amendments in 2023

As the PMLA Amendments of 2023 align with the RBI Directions, it has become mandatory for registered entities that utilize the cloud deployment model to follow some additional guidelines.

When the cloud deployment model is employed, it is imperative that the ownership of data in this model resides solely with the RE. All data, including video recordings, must be promptly transferred to the RE's exclusively owned or leased servers, including any cloud server, immediately after the completion of the V-CIP process. The cloud service provider or third-party technology provider assisting the V-CIP of the RE should not retain any data.

The V-CIP records and data must be securely stored in India, in compliance with record management instructions, and subject to concurrent audit.

Any form of disruption, such as video pauses or call reconnections, should not result in the creation of multiple video files. If a pause or disruption does not lead to the creation of multiple files, there is no need for the RE to initiate a fresh session. However, in the event of a call drop or disconnection, a fresh session should be initiated.

CDD FOR SOLE PROPRIETORS

For opening an account in the name of a sole proprietary firm, the CDD process includes verifying the identity of the individual proprietor. Additionally, at least two documents or their electronic equivalents that serve as proof of business or activity under the name of the proprietary firm should be obtained.

The acceptable documents include the registration certificate, issued by the government, certificates/licenses issued by municipal authorities, sales and income tax returns, CST/VAT/GST certificate, certificates/registration documents issued by tax authorities, Importer Exporter Code (IEC), and complete income tax returns in the name of the sole proprietor. Utility bills like electricity, water, and landline telephone bills can also be considered.

In cases where it is not possible to furnish two documents, the reporting entities (REs) have the discretion to accept only one document as proof of business/activity. However, REs must conduct contact point verification, collect additional information, and seek clarifications to establish the existence of the firm. They should also confirm that the business activity has been verified from the address of the proprietary concern.

In the amendments done in 2023, Udyam Registration Certificate (URC) issued by the Government will now be considered as the valid documentation of KYC. The Udyam Registration Certificate (URC) is a certificate issued by the government of India under the Micro, Small, and Medium Enterprises Development (MSMED) Act, 2006.

It is a registration process for small and medium-sized enterprises (SMEs) that provides them with certain benefits and recognition. The URC is a proof of registration and helps SMEs avail various government schemes, subsidies, and other support programs. It serves as a document that confirms the status of a business as a micro, small, or medium enterprise.

CDD FOR LEGAL ENTITIES

For opening an account of a company, the following documents are required: certificate of incorporation, memorandum and articles of association, permanent account number of the company, a resolution from the board of directors and power of attorney, documents relating to beneficial owners, names of relevant persons holding senior management position, and registered office details.

For opening an account of a partnership firm, the required documents include: registration certificate, partnership deed, permanent account number of the partnership firm, documents relating to beneficial owners, names of all partners, and address details.

For opening an account of a trust, the necessary documents are: registration certificate, trust deed, permanent account number or Form No.60 of the trust, documents relating to beneficial owners, names of beneficiaries, trustees, settlor, and authors of the trust, and address details.

For opening an account of an unincorporated association or body of individuals, the required documents include: resolution of the managing body, permanent account number or Form No.60 of the association or body, power of attorney, documents relating to beneficial owners, and any additional information required to establish its legal existence.

For opening an account of a juridical person (such as societies, universities, local bodies), the necessary documents include: document showing the authorized person's name, documents relating to persons holding power of attorney, and any additional documents required to establish the legal existence of the entity/juridical person.

Amendments in 2023

The amendments in the RBI Directives include the following additional requirements:

In addition to the KYC documents mentioned in the RBI Master Directions, the names of relevant persons holding senior management positions is necessary in case of company. Providing the registered office and principal place of business (if different) is also needed.

For opening an account of a partnership firm, the names of all partners and the address of the registered office and principal place of business (if different) are required.

For opening an account of a trust, the names of beneficiaries, trustees, settlor, and authors of the trust must be provided. Additionally, the address of the registered office of the trust and a list of trustees, along with specified documents, are necessary for those discharging the role as a trustee and authorized to transact on behalf of the trust.

ULTIMATE BENEFICIAL OWNER

The ultimate beneficial owner refers to the individual(s) who ultimately owns or controls a legal entity or has the ultimate authority over its operations, management, and decision-making.

This includes individuals who have a significant ownership interest or exercise control through other means such as voting rights or contractual agreements.

UBOS IN COMPANY

The beneficial owner of a company is the natural person(s) who, individually or collectively with others, possesses a controlling ownership interest or exercises control through other methods. A "controlling ownership interest" is defined as ownership of or entitlement to more than 25 percent of the shares, capital, or profits of the company. However, in 2023, the rules were amended, and companies are now required to disclose information about any shareholder holding more than 10 percent of the shares. Control may involve the authority to appoint a majority of directors or influence management and policy decisions.

UBOS IN FIRMS

For a partnership firm, the beneficial owner is the natural person(s) who, alone or together with others, holds ownership of or entitlement to more than 15 percent of the capital or profits of the partnership.

UBOS OF AOP/BOI

In the case of an unincorporated association or body of individuals, the beneficial owner is the natural person(s) who, either alone or together with others, holds ownership of or entitlement to more than 15 percent of the property, capital, or profits of the association or body of individuals.

If no natural person is identified as the beneficial owner in the aforementioned cases, the relevant natural person holding the position of senior managing official is considered the beneficial owner.

In the case of a trust, identifying the beneficial owner(s) includes identifying the author of the trust, the trustee, beneficiaries with a 10 percent or more interest in the trust, and any other natural person exercising ultimate effective control over the trust through a chain of control or ownership.

EXCEPTION OF UBO IDENTIFICATION

According to the regulations, when opening an account for a legal person that is not a natural person, it is important to identify and verify the identity of the beneficial owner.

However, there are exceptions to this requirement for certain entities. If the customer or the owner of the controlling interest is a listed entity on an Indian stock exchange, or a resident entity in jurisdictions specified by the Central Government and listed on stock exchanges in those jurisdictions, or a subsidiary of such listed entities, there is no need to identify and verify the identity of any shareholder or beneficial owner of those entities.

ON GOING DUE DILIGENCE

According to the guidelines, reporting entities (REs) are required to conduct ongoing due diligence of their customers to ensure that their transactions align with the REs' knowledge about the customers, their business, risk profile, and the source of funds. Certain types of transactions, such as large and complex transactions, transactions with unusual patterns inconsistent with normal activity, and transactions exceeding prescribed thresholds, must be closely monitored. REs should also pay attention to high account turnover and the deposit of third-party cheques followed by large cash withdrawals.

To enhance the effectiveness of ongoing due diligence, REs are encouraged to adopt innovative technologies like artificial intelligence and machine learning. The level of monitoring should be proportionate to the risk category of the customer, with high-risk accounts requiring more intensified monitoring. REs must establish a system for periodic review of account risk categorization, conducted at least once every six months, and implement enhanced due diligence measures as necessary.

Specific attention should be given to transactions involving marketing firms, particularly accounts of Multi-level Marketing (MLM) Companies, which should be closely monitored. Instances where a large number of cheque books are requested, multiple small cash deposits are made across different locations in a single bank account, or numerous cheques are issued with similar amounts and dates should be immediately reported to the Reserve Bank of India and other relevant authorities, such as FIU-IND.

UPDATING KYC

The RBI circular RBI/DBR/2015-16/18, Master Direction DBR.AML.BC.No.81/14.01.001/2015-16, provides guidelines for the periodic updation of KYC (Know Your Customer) for reporting entities (REs). The circular emphasizes a risk-based approach for periodic updation, with different frequencies based on the risk profile of customers. It highlights the requirements for individuals and customers other than

KYC COMPLIANCE AND REGULATORY FRAMEWORK

individuals in terms of KYC information updates and verification processes.

For individuals, if there are no changes in the KYC information, a self-declaration from the customer is obtained through various channels like email, mobile number, ATMs, or digital platforms. In case of a change in the address, a self-declaration of the new address is obtained, and verification is done within two months. The circular also addresses the updation of accounts for customers who were minors at the time of opening, and the use of Aadhaar OTP-based e-KYC for periodic updation.

For customers other than individuals, self-declaration is obtained for no change in KYC information, and in case of changes, the KYC process equivalent to onboarding a new customer is undertaken. REs are also required to ensure the availability and accuracy of KYC documents and Beneficial Ownership (BO) information. Additional measures include verifying PAN details, providing acknowledgments to customers, promptly updating information in records, and offering convenience for periodic KYC updation.

REs are encouraged to adopt a risk-based approach and may implement additional measures beyond the mandated instructions based on their internal KYC policy, duly approved by the Board of Directors or a delegated committee. The circular aims to ensure compliance with KYC requirements and periodic updating while providing flexibility for REs to address specific risks and customer convenience.

Amendments in 2023

As per the amendments in 2023, reporting entities (REs) are required to inform customers about the need to comply with PML (Prevention of Money Laundering) Rules. In case there are any changes or updates to the documents provided by the customer during the establishment of the business relationship or account-based relationship, customers must submit the updated documents to the REs. This should be done within 30 days of the update in order to ensure that the records at the REs' end are kept up to date.

The amendments made to the RBI Master direction in 2023 introduce Enhanced Due Diligence (EDD) requirements for non-face-to-face customer onboarding. Non-face-to-face onboarding allows reporting entities (REs) to establish relationships with customers without meeting them physically or through video customer identification process (V-CIP). This includes the use of digital channels such as CKYCR, DigiLocker, and equivalent e-documents, as well as non-digital methods like obtaining a copy of officially valid documents (OVDs) certified by additional certifying authorities. The following EDD measures must be undertaken by REs for non-face-to-face customer onboarding:

a) REs that have implemented V-CIP must provide it as the first option for remote onboarding. V-CIP processes that comply with prescribed standards and procedures are treated equivalent to face-to-face customer identification process (CIP) in this Master Direction.

b) To prevent fraud, alternate mobile numbers cannot be linked to such accounts for transaction-related purposes after customer due diligence (CDD) is completed. Transactions can only be conducted from the mobile number used for account opening. REs should have a board-approved policy for handling requests to change registered mobile numbers.

c) In addition to obtaining proof of the current address, REs must verify the current address through positive confirmation before allowing operations in the account. Positive confirmation can be done through methods such as address verification letter, contact point verification, and deliverables.

d) REs must obtain the customer's PAN (Permanent Account Number) and verify it using the verification facility provided by the issuing authority.

e) The first transaction in such accounts must be a credit from the customer's existing KYC-compliant bank account.

f) Customers onboarded through non-face-to-face mode are considered high-risk customers and their accounts are subject to enhanced monitoring until their identity is verified through face-to-face interaction or V-CIP.

KYC AUDITS AND INSPECTIONS

KYC audits and inspections refer to the processes and procedures carried out by regulatory authorities or internal compliance teams to assess the effectiveness and compliance of an organization's Know Your Customer (KYC) practices. These audits and inspections aim to ensure that the organization is following the required KYC guidelines and regulations to mitigate risks associated with money laundering, terrorism financing, fraud, and other financial crimes.

During a KYC audit or inspection, the regulatory authority or internal compliance team reviews the organization's KYC policies, procedures, and practices to verify their adequacy and adherence to applicable laws and regulations. The audit or inspection may involve the following activities:

1. Documentation Review: The auditors or inspectors examine the organization's KYC policies, procedures, and documentation related to customer due diligence, identity verification, risk assessment, and record-keeping. They assess whether the organization has established comprehensive and well-documented KYC processes.

2. Process Evaluation: The auditors or inspectors assess how the organization implements its KYC procedures and whether they are followed consistently across the organization. They may review the customer onboarding process, KYC data collection, verification methods, risk assessment practices, and ongoing monitoring of customer accounts.

3. Compliance Assessment: The auditors or inspectors verify whether the organization is compliant with relevant regulatory requirements, industry standards, and internal policies. They check if the organization has identified and implemented necessary measures to address KYC risks and whether appropriate controls are in place to prevent money laundering and other illicit activities.

4. Testing and Sampling: The auditors or inspectors may select a sample of customer files or transactions to test the organization's KYC practices. They review the accuracy and completeness of customer information, assess the effectiveness of identity verification methods, and evaluate the organization's risk assessment and mitigation processes.

5. Reporting and Recommendations: After the audit or inspection, the regulatory authority or internal compliance team provides a detailed report highlighting any deficiencies or non-compliance identified during the process. They may also provide recommendations or suggestions for improving the organization's KYC processes and strengthening compliance measures.

Audit refers to the process of evaluating the extent to which a system or company complies with a set of standards, which can be defined by laws or regulations. It involves a systematic review of the company's practices and procedures in comparison to the requirements set by the standards. Here are some examples of what an audit may assess:

The first point in a KYC audit is to assess whether the company has a board-approved KYC policy. This involves reviewing the company's documented policies and procedures related to customer identification and due diligence. The audit team examines if the policy is in line with regulatory requirements, clearly defines the processes for verifying customer identities, and outlines the steps to be taken in case of non-compliance. A board-approved policy demonstrates the company's commitment to implementing effective KYC measures.

Another crucial aspect of a KYC audit is to evaluate the presence of a customer acceptance and identification policy (CAP/CIP). The audit team reviews this policy to ensure it covers the necessary steps for accepting and identifying customers, such as verifying their identity documents, conducting risk assessments, and determining customer eligibility. The policy should be comprehensive, well-documented, and aligned with industry best practices and regulatory guidelines.

During a KYC audit, the methods and identifiers used by the company for its KYC program are examined. This involves assessing the various tools, systems, and processes employed to collect and verify customer information. The audit team reviews the effectiveness and reliability of these methods, such as document verification, biometric authentication, or data matching with external databases. The goal is to ensure that the company utilizes robust and reliable mechanisms to authenticate customer identities.

The audit team analyzes the customer profiles or mandates against the established standards. They assess how many of these profiles comply with the required KYC measures and how many do not. Additionally, the audit identifies non-compliant profiles that pose a material or non-material risk. This evaluation helps determine the level of risk exposure for the company and enables them to prioritize remedial actions for the non-compliant profiles.

In a KYC audit, the storage and management of KYC records for future reference are assessed. The audit team examines how the company maintains customer data securely, ensuring confidentiality, integrity, and availability. They evaluate the storage infrastructure, data retention policies, access controls, and measures taken to protect customer information from unauthorized access or loss. Proper record-keeping is crucial for regulatory compliance, investigations, and customer relationship management.

The KYC audit scrutinizes the company's classification and handling of high-risk politically exposed persons (PEPs). The audit team identifies the number of clients categorized as PEPs and reviews the company's procedures for conducting enhanced due diligence on such individuals. They also assess the company's awareness of the jurisdictions in which these high-risk clients are based, as this information plays a vital role in assessing potential risks associated with money laundering or corruption.

The effectiveness of the KYC software utilized by the company is evaluated during the audit. The audit team assesses the software's functionality, accuracy, and reliability in performing customer identification and verification processes. They also review the scripting used in the software to ensure it aligns with regulatory requirements and industry best practices. Additionally, the audit team examines the occurrence of false positive results, as an excessive number of false positives may indicate inefficiencies or potential gaps in the KYC software's performance, which could lead to missed risks or additional workload for the compliance team.

The purpose of KYC audits and inspections is to ensure that organizations have robust KYC frameworks in place, comply with regulatory requirements, and mitigate the risks associated with financial crimes. By conducting regular audits and inspections, regulatory authorities and organizations can identify areas for improvement, rectify deficiencies, and enhance the overall effectiveness of their KYC practices.

CHALLENGES IN KYC COMPLIANCE

India has a complex regulatory environment with multiple regulatory bodies overseeing different sectors. Each regulatory body may have its own KYC requirements, leading to variations in compliance procedures. Keeping up with the evolving regulations and ensuring alignment with all applicable rules can be challenging for businesses.

• Large Customer Base: India has a vast population, making customer identification and verification a challenging task. Conducting KYC procedures for a large number of customers within a reasonable timeframe can be time-consuming and resource-intensive. It requires robust systems and processes to handle the volume while maintaining accuracy and efficiency.

• Diversity in Documentation: India is a diverse country with various identity documents and address proofs accepted for KYC purposes. The challenge lies in verifying the authenticity of different types of documents and ensuring consistency in the verification process. Additionally, verifying documents from rural areas or remote regions can be more challenging due to limited access to technology and infrastructure.

- Technological Infrastructure: Implementing effective KYC compliance requires a robust technological infrastructure capable of handling data securely, conducting verification processes, and managing customer records. Some areas in India may have limited internet connectivity or technological resources, which can hinder the smooth implementation of digital KYC solutions.
- Data Privacy and Security: KYC compliance involves collecting and storing sensitive customer information, which raises concerns about data privacy and security. It is essential to establish robust data protection measures and ensure compliance with data privacy regulations to safeguard customer data from unauthorized access or breaches.
- Cost and Resource Allocation: Implementing and maintaining a comprehensive KYC compliance program can be expensive. It requires investments in technology, training, and skilled personnel to ensure effective compliance. Small and medium-sized enterprises may face challenges in allocating sufficient resources for KYC compliance, which can impact their ability to meet regulatory requirements.
- Rapidly Changing Technology and Fraud Techniques: Technology advancements have led to the emergence of sophisticated fraud techniques, necessitating continuous updates to KYC systems and processes. Staying abreast of technological advancements and evolving fraud patterns is crucial to detect and prevent fraudulent activities effectively.
- Customer Experience: While ensuring compliance, organizations must also focus on providing a smooth and seamless customer experience during the KYC process.

Balancing stringent compliance requirements with customer convenience and satisfaction can be challenging, as customers expect quick and hassle-free onboarding procedures.

CHALLENGES FACED BY REGULATED ENTITIES

Regulated entities, such as banks, financial institutions, and other organizations subject to KYC compliance, encounter several challenges in meeting the requirements

a) High cost and resource burden: Implementing and maintaining effective KYC processes can be expensive and resource-intensive for regulated entities. It involves investing in technology, hiring skilled personnel, and continuously monitoring and updating customer information.

b) Complex regulatory landscape: The ever-evolving regulatory landscape adds complexity to KYC compliance. Regulated entities must stay updated with changing regulations, guidelines, and industry best practices. Adapting their processes and systems to meet new requirements can be challenging.

c) Balancing compliance and customer experience: Striking a balance between strict compliance measures and providing a seamless customer experience is a challenge. Stringent KYC procedures may create friction in customer onboarding and transactions, potentially leading to customer dissatisfaction or abandonment.

CHALLENGES FACED BY CUSTOMERS

Customers also face certain challenges when undergoing the KYC process

a) Inconvenience and time-consuming: Providing extensive documentation, visiting physical branches, or undergoing repeated verification processes can be inconvenient and time-consuming for customers. Lengthy procedures may discourage potential customers or delay access to financial services.

b) Privacy and data security concerns: Customers may have concerns about the privacy and security of their personal information during the KYC process. They may worry about data breaches or misuse of their information, leading to identity theft or fraud.

c) Lack of uniformity: Different regulated entities may have varying KYC requirements and procedures, leading to confusion and duplication of efforts for customers. This lack of uniformity adds to the complexity and inconvenience of the KYC process.

CHALLENGES FACED BY THE GOVERNMENT

The government faces specific challenges in implementing and overseeing the KYC framework

a) Coordination and information sharing: Government agencies responsible for KYC oversight need to ensure effective coordination and information sharing among different entities and sectors. This includes sharing data and intelligence to identify and prevent money laundering, terrorist financing, and other financial crimes.

b) Enforcement and monitoring: Monitoring and enforcing compliance across a wide range of regulated entities and sectors pose challenges. Government agencies need to allocate resources, conduct audits and inspections, and take appropriate actions against non-compliant entities.

c) Technological advancements: Keeping pace with technological advancements is a challenge for the government. Criminals are constantly finding new ways to exploit technology for illicit activities, necessitating the government to adopt advanced tools and techniques to detect and prevent financial crimes.

ADDRESSING THE CHALLENGES

To address the challenges in KYC compliance, various measures can be taken

a) Streamlining processes: Regulated entities can streamline their KYC processes by leveraging technology, implementing automation, and adopting risk-based approaches. This can help reduce costs, improve efficiency, and enhance the customer experience.

b) Standardization and harmonization: Encouraging standardization and harmonization of KYC requirements across different sectors can simplify the process for customers and regulated entities. This includes promoting the use of common standards, documentation, and technology platforms.

c) Enhancing data security and privacy: Regulated entities should prioritize data security and privacy by implementing robust safeguards, encryption measures, and strict access controls. Clear communication with customers about data protection measures can help build trust and alleviate concerns.

d) Collaboration and information sharing: Government agencies, regulated entities, and other stakeholders should collaborate and share information effectively to combat financial crimes. This includes establishing centralized databases, developing information-sharing platforms, and fostering a culture of cooperation.

e) Continuous training and awareness: Regular training and awareness programs for regulated entities and customers can enhance understanding of KYC requirements and best practices. This can help ensure compliance and enable customers to navigate the KYC process more effectively.

By addressing these challenges, stakeholders can work towards achieving effective KYC compliance, mitigating financial risks, and maintaining the integrity of the financial system.

KYC AND DIGITAL TRANSFORMATION

Digital transformation refers to the integration of digital technologies into various aspects of business operations, including the Know Your Customer (KYC) process. KYC is a crucial requirement in many industries, especially in the financial sector, to verify the identity of customers and assess potential risks associated with them. Digital transformation in KYC involves leveraging technology and digital solutions to streamline and enhance the KYC process.

Digital transformation in the context of Know Your Customer (KYC) refers to the integration of digital technologies and processes into the traditional KYC procedures. It involves leveraging technology to digitize and automate various aspects of the KYC process, enabling organizations to streamline operations, enhance customer experience, and improve efficiency.

In a traditional KYC process, customer identification, verification, and risk assessment are typically carried out manually, involving physical documents, paperwork, and face-to-face interactions. However, with digital transformation, organizations adopt digital solutions and technologies to digitize, automate, and enhance these processes.

Digital transformation in KYC can involve various technological advancements, such as:

ROLE OF TECHNOLOGY IN KYC

Technology plays a significant role in modernizing and improving the KYC process. It enables automation, data analysis, and faster information exchange, leading to a more efficient and cost-effective KYC process. Various technologies such as artificial intelligence (AI), machine learning (ML), biometrics, and data analytics are used to enhance customer identification, verification, and risk assessment in KYC.

ONLINE FORMS AND DOCUMENT SUBMISSION

Online forms and document submission refers to the use of digital platforms and applications where customers can provide their personal information and upload electronic copies of their identification documents instead of using traditional paper-based forms and physically submitting physical documents.

In the traditional process, when a customer goes through a KYC process, they are typically required to fill out paper forms manually, providing details such as their name, address, contact information, and other relevant information. They are also required to provide physical copies of identification documents such as passports, driver's licenses, or identity cards.

However, with online forms and document submission, this process is digitized. Customers can access a secure online platform or application provided by the organization conducting the KYC process. They are presented with digital forms that they can fill out electronically, entering their information directly into the online system.

Instead of submitting physical copies of their identification documents, customers can scan or take high-quality photographs of their documents and upload them digitally to the online platform. This can be done through various methods such as uploading files from their computer or mobile device, or taking pictures using the camera on their device.

The digital forms and uploaded documents are securely stored and processed by the organization conducting the KYC process. This eliminates the need for customers to physically visit a location or send their documents through mail or in-person visits.

By adopting online forms and document submission, the KYC process becomes more convenient and efficient for customers. They can complete the necessary forms and submit their identification documents from the comfort of their own homes or any location with internet access. It reduces the need for manual data entry, eliminates the risk of document loss, and accelerates the overall KYC process.

For organizations, online forms and document submission streamline the data collection and verification process. It enables faster processing, reduces manual errors, and provides a digital record of customer information, making it easier to retrieve and analyze when needed.

Electronic Identity Verification:

Technologies like biometrics, facial recognition, and digital identity verification services are employed to authenticate customers' identities remotely and in real-time.

DATA ANALYTICS AND ARTIFICIAL INTELLIGENCE (AI)

In the context of KYC, data analytics and artificial intelligence (AI) are used together to analyze customer data, identify patterns, and assess risks related to individuals or entities. Here's a further elaboration:

Data Analytics: Data analytics involves analyzing large volumes of customer data to extract meaningful insights and patterns. In KYC, organizations collect various types of customer information, such as personal details, financial records, transaction history, and behavior patterns. By applying data analytics techniques, such as statistical analysis and machine learning algorithms, organizations can process and analyze this data to identify patterns, trends, and anomalies. For example, they can detect unusual transaction patterns or identify correlations between certain customer behaviors and potential risks.

Artificial Intelligence (AI): AI refers to the development of computer systems capable of performing tasks that typically require human intelligence, such as learning, reasoning, and decision-making. In the context of KYC, AI algorithms are employed to automate certain aspects of the process and enhance risk assessment capabilities. AI-powered systems can analyze vast amounts of customer data, apply predefined rules and algorithms, and make intelligent decisions or predictions. For instance, AI algorithms can automatically flag suspicious activities, identify potential fraud indicators, or generate risk scores for individuals or entities based on their data profiles.

Combining Data Analytics and AI: By combining data analytics and AI, organizations can leverage advanced algorithms and techniques to process and analyze customer data more efficiently and effectively. AI algorithms can identify hidden patterns, detect anomalies, and generate insights that might not be apparent through traditional analysis methods. This can help organizations in the KYC process by improving the accuracy of risk assessment, reducing false positives, and identifying potential risks or fraudulent activities with greater precision.

ELECTRONIC DATA SOURCES

In the context of digital transformation in KYC, electronic data sources refer to external databases and digital platforms that provide relevant information about individuals or entities during the customer verification process. These sources are integrated into the KYC systems of organizations to gather information and validate customer details more efficiently and accurately.

Electronic data sources can include various types of databases and platforms, such as:

Government Databases: Organizations can integrate with government databases that contain official records, such as identity documents, passports, driver's licenses, or national identification databases. This integration allows for quick and reliable verification of customer-provided information against official records.

Credit Bureaus: Credit bureaus maintain extensive data on individuals' credit history, financial transactions, and creditworthiness. By integrating with credit bureaus' databases, organizations can access credit reports and other relevant financial information to assess the creditworthiness and risk associated with customers.

Watchlists and Sanctions Lists: Integration with watchlists and sanctions lists maintained by regulatory bodies and international organizations allows organizations to screen customers against known criminal or sanctioned entities. This helps identify individuals or entities involved in illegal activities or subject to sanctions.

Identity Verification Services: There are specialized identity verification services that provide access to a wide range of data sources, such as public records, utility bills, social media profiles, and more. These services utilize advanced algorithms and data analytics techniques to gather and analyze data, providing organizations with comprehensive identity verification capabilities.

Online Data Sources: Organizations can leverage various online data sources, including social media platforms, professional networks, public forums, and online news articles, to gather additional information about customers. This information can be used to supplement the verification process and gain further insights into customer backgrounds.

By integrating with these electronic data sources, organizations can gather relevant information more efficiently and effectively during the KYC process. This integration allows for real-time data retrieval, reducing the need for manual verification and minimizing the chances of human error. It enables organizations to validate customer details, cross-reference information, and assess risks more accurately.

Electronic Data Sources in India

In past few years, India has advanced its database capabilities. These databases serve different purpose and in various domains you get different databases. It is important to know some of the most important databases in different sectors. KYC is not only limited to Banking and Finance sector. It is spreading its wing across different sectors and these databases are going to be crucial. There are many regtech companies which are working on these datasets.

In India, several databases play a crucial role in various sectors, including finance, governance, and identification. Here are some notable databases in India:

1. Aadhaar Database: Aadhaar is a unique identification system in India that assigns a 12-digit unique identification number to residents based on their biometric and demographic data. The Aadhaar database contains information such as name, address, date of birth, and biometric records of individuals. It is used for identity verification and authentication purposes across various sectors.
2. PAN Database: PAN (Permanent Account Number) is a unique alphanumeric identifier issued by the Income Tax Department of India. The PAN database contains details of individuals and entities who hold PAN cards,

including their names, addresses, and tax-related information. It is primarily used for income tax purposes and financial transactions.
3. Credit Information Companies: Credit information companies such as Credit Information Bureau India Limited (CIBIL), Experian, Equifax, and TransUnion maintain databases that contain credit histories and financial information of individuals and entities. These databases help lenders and financial institutions assess creditworthiness, track credit histories, and make informed decisions regarding loans and financial services.
4. National Population Register (NPR): The National Population Register is a comprehensive database that aims to create a list of usual residents of India. It collects demographic data such as name, gender, age, and address of individuals. The NPR database serves as a foundation for various government initiatives and policies.
5. Securities and Exchange Board of India (SEBI) Database: SEBI maintains databases that include information related to securities markets, registered entities, market intermediaries, and investor-related data. These databases assist in regulating and monitoring activities in the securities market, ensuring compliance with securities laws and regulations.
6. Reserve Bank of India (RBI) Database: The RBI maintains several databases related to banking and finance. These databases include information on banks, financial institutions, non-banking financial

companies, and other regulated entities. They help the RBI in supervising and regulating the banking sector and formulating monetary policies.
7. Voter ID Database[ix]: The Election Commission of India maintains the voter ID database, which contains voter information, including name, address, and unique voter identification number. This database is used for electoral processes, including voter registration, electoral roll management, and conducting elections.
8. National Crime Records Bureau (NCRB) Database: The NCRB maintains a database of criminal records and crime statistics in India. It collects and analyzes data related to crimes, criminals, and law enforcement agencies. This database aids in monitoring and addressing crime patterns, supporting law enforcement agencies, and formulating crime prevention strategies.
9. National Automated Clearing House (NACH) Database: NACH is a centralized payment system managed by the National Payments Corporation of India (NPCI). It maintains a database of bank account details, including account numbers and associated customer information. The NACH database facilitates automated electronic transactions such as direct debit and direct credit.
10. Central Know Your Customer (CKYC) Database: The CKYC database is maintained by the Central Registry of Securitization and Asset Reconstruction and Security Interest of India (CERSAI). It is used for storing and sharing KYC information of customers across financial institutions, including banks, mutual

funds, insurance companies, and other entities. The database helps streamline and standardize the KYC process, reducing duplication of efforts and enhancing customer convenience.

11. National Health Data Warehouse (NHDW): The NHDW is an initiative by the Ministry of Health and Family Welfare in India to consolidate health-related data from various sources. It aims to establish a comprehensive database for healthcare planning, research, and policy-making purposes. The NHDW includes information on health facilities, disease patterns, and patient data, among other health-related parameters.

12. Goods and Services Tax Network (GSTN) Database: The GSTN database is a centralized system that stores data related to Goods and Services Tax (GST) in India. It maintains information about businesses, their GST registrations, tax filings, and transaction details. The GSTN database facilitates the administration and compliance of the GST regime.

13. National Securities Depository Limited (NSDL) Database: NSDL is a depository that holds securities such as stocks, bonds, and other financial instruments in electronic form. The NSDL database maintains records of dematerialized securities, investor details, and transaction history. It facilitates efficient and secure trading and settlement of securities.

14. National Judicial Data Grid (NJDG) Database[x]: The NJDG is an online repository of case information from district courts, high courts, and the Supreme Court of India. It provides access to details of pending and

disposed of cases, case status, case history, and other relevant information. The NJDG database helps in tracking and monitoring court cases and enhances transparency in the judicial system.

15. Indian Patent Office Database: The Indian Patent Office maintains a database of patents granted in India. It contains information about the inventors, patent applicants, patent titles, and patent specifications. The database supports innovation and research by providing access to existing patents and facilitating patent searches.

16. National Land Records Database[xi]: The National Land Records Database, also known as the Land Records Management Information System (LRMIS), stores land-related information such as property ownership records, land surveys, and land transaction details. It aids in maintaining land records, preventing land disputes, and facilitating property transactions.

17. Drug Controller General of India (DCGI) Database: The DCGI database maintains information related to pharmaceuticals, clinical trials, and drug regulatory approvals in India. It includes details about drug manufacturers, drug formulations, drug safety data, and other relevant information. The database supports the regulation and oversight of the pharmaceutical industry.

18. National Automated Fingerprints Identification System (NAFIS) Database[xii]: NAFIS is a centralized fingerprint database managed by the National Crime Records Bureau. It stores fingerprint records of individuals collected by law enforcement agencies.

The database helps in identifying and verifying individuals involved in criminal investigations.

19. Central Vehicle Registry Database: The Central Vehicle Registry database contains information related to motor vehicles registered in India. It includes details such as vehicle identification numbers (VINs), registration numbers, ownership records, and vehicle specifications. The database helps in vehicle identification, ownership verification, and tracking stolen vehicles[xiii].

20. Indian Railway Catering and Tourism Corporation (IRCTC) Database: The IRCTC database stores passenger information related to train bookings and reservations in India. It includes details such as passenger names, contact information, journey details, and ticketing records. The database facilitates the efficient management of railway bookings and passenger services.

21. National Skills Registry (NSR) Database: NSR is a centralized repository of employee background information and skill sets in India. It stores data such as educational qualifications, employment history, and professional certifications of individuals. The database helps organizations verify and validate employee credentials during recruitment and background checks.[xiv]

22. Unique Disability ID (UDID) Database[xv]: The UDID database is a unique identification system for persons with disabilities in India. It stores information about individuals with disabilities, including their personal details, disability type, and support requirements. The

database aids in providing targeted services, schemes, and entitlements for persons with disabilities.
23. Central Registry of Securitization Asset Reconstruction and Security Interest (CERSAI) Database[xvi]: CERSAI maintains a registry of security interests on movable and immovable properties created for loans and other financial transactions. The database helps in verifying property ownership, preventing fraud, and facilitating secured lending.
24. Centralized Public Grievance Redress and Monitoring System (CPGRAMS) Database [xvii] : CPGRAMS is an online platform for citizens to lodge complaints and grievances with various government departments and agencies. The database records and tracks the status of complaints, facilitating timely redressal and monitoring of grievances.
25. National Knowledge Network (NKN) Database[xviii]: The NKN is a high-speed network that connects educational and research institutions across India. It enables the exchange of information, collaboration, and access to databases and research resources in various disciplines.

These are the top 25 databases where a significant information related to the person's KYC is stored. There are many other corporate databases which can also be integrated with the KYC verification systems.

WORKFLOW AUTOMATION

Workflow automation refers to the implementation of automated tools and processes to streamline and expedite the Know Your Customer (KYC) process. It involves leveraging technology to reduce manual interventions, simplify tasks, and improve the overall efficiency of the KYC process.

In a traditional KYC process, there are numerous manual steps involved, such as collecting customer information, verifying documents, conducting background checks, and performing risk assessments. These manual tasks can be time-consuming, prone to errors, and may require significant human intervention.

With workflow automation, organizations use technology solutions to automate these tasks and create a structured and efficient workflow. Here's how it works:

Task Assignment and Prioritization

Task assignment and prioritization automation refers to the use of software or tools to automatically assign tasks to appropriate team members based on predefined rules and priorities. Instead of manually assigning tasks, automation streamlines the process by intelligently distributing tasks to the most suitable individuals or teams.

The automation tools are programmed with predefined rules and criteria that determine which team members should be assigned specific tasks. These rules can take into account factors such as workload, expertise, availability, or specific skill requirements. For example, if a task requires knowledge in a particular area, the automation tool can assign it to team members who possess the necessary expertise in that domain.

Prioritization is another important aspect of task assignment automation. The automation tool can assign priorities to tasks based on their urgency, importance, or specific deadlines. This ensures that critical tasks are given higher priority and are assigned to team members accordingly. By automating the prioritization process, it becomes more efficient and reduces the risk of tasks being overlooked or delayed due to human error. The benefits of task assignment and prioritization automation include:

- Efficiency: Automation eliminates the need for manual task assignment, saving time and reducing administrative overhead. It allows team members to focus on executing tasks rather than spending time on assigning them.
- Fairness and Transparency: Automation ensures a fair distribution of tasks among team members based on predefined rules and criteria. It removes biases or subjective judgment in task assignment, promoting transparency and equal opportunities for team members.
- Optimization of Resources: By intelligently assigning tasks based on workload and expertise, automation helps optimize resource allocation. It ensures that tasks are assigned to individuals who have the capacity and skill set to complete them efficiently.
- Timeliness: Prioritization automation ensures that critical tasks are assigned and completed on time. It helps in meeting deadlines and avoiding bottlenecks or delays in task execution.
- Scalability: Automation tools can handle large volumes of tasks and adapt to changing workload demands. This scalability ensures that as the volume of tasks increases, the automation system can efficiently distribute and manage them without compromising productivity.
- Document Digitization and Extraction: Automation can help convert physical documents into digital format,

allowing for easier storage, retrieval, and analysis. It can also extract relevant data from documents using Optical Character Recognition (OCR) technology, reducing the need for manual data entry.

- Data Validation and Verification: Automation tools can perform automated checks and validations on customer data, ensuring its accuracy and completeness. It can compare the provided information with external databases and sources to verify customer details.

- Rules-Based Decision Making: Automation allows organizations to define rules and algorithms that guide decision-making processes. For example, certain criteria can be set to flag high-risk customers or trigger additional verification steps.

- Notification and Collaboration: Automation tools can send notifications and alerts to the relevant stakeholders when specific actions are required. It facilitates communication and collaboration between team members, ensuring timely completion of tasks.

The goal of workflow automation in digital transformation of KYC is to enhance the efficiency and effectiveness of the process. By automating repetitive and time-consuming tasks, organizations can reduce processing time, minimize errors, and improve the overall accuracy of customer data. It also enables organizations to comply with regulatory requirements more effectively by ensuring consistent application of rules and procedures.

ADVANTAGES OF DIGITAL KYC

Digital KYC offers several advantages over traditional manual processes:

- Efficiency: Digital KYC reduces manual paperwork and administrative tasks, allowing for faster and streamlined onboarding of customers.
- Enhanced Customer Experience: Digital KYC enables a seamless and convenient customer onboarding experience, reducing the need for physical document submission and in-person visits.
- Improved Accuracy: Technology-driven KYC processes minimize human errors and improve the accuracy of customer data collection and verification.
- Cost Savings: Digital KYC reduces operational costs associated with manual processes, such as physical document storage, printing, and staff resources.
- Compliance and Risk Mitigation: Digital KYC solutions help organizations adhere to regulatory requirements by implementing robust identity verification and risk assessment procedures.

RISKS AND CHALLENGES IN KYC

Many firms have invested in digital transformation to streamline their customer onboarding processes. However, despite these efforts, they often struggle with inefficient processes and end up wasting significant amounts of money and man-hours when it comes to ongoing KYC monitoring. KYC monitoring is crucial for ensuring compliance with Money Laundering directives and preventing financial crimes.

The inefficiencies in ongoing monitoring can be attributed to various factors. One common issue is the presence of manual and time-consuming processes that rely heavily on human intervention. These processes may involve manual data entry, manual document verification, and manual review of customer profiles, which can be prone to errors and delays. As a result, firms end up spending excessive time and resources on repetitive tasks that could be automated.

Many companies face challenges in complying with Know Your Customer (KYC) regulations in India.

Here are seven common pain points and suggested solutions:

FALSE POSITIVES

False positives in the context of KYC monitoring refer to situations where a genuine customer is flagged for further scrutiny or enhanced due diligence based on matches with names on political exposed persons (PEPs) or sanctions lists. These matches can occur due to similarities in names, which may trigger alerts for potential risk or suspicious activity.

Dealing with false positives can be a significant challenge for firms as it consumes valuable time and resources. Investigations need to be conducted to determine whether the flagged customer poses an actual risk or if it was a false alarm. These investigations may involve manual verification of documents, gathering additional information, and potentially engaging in time-consuming communication with the customer to clarify their identity and intent.

Implementing automated processes can help address this issue by reducing the number of false positives and minimizing the associated operational costs. Automated systems can employ advanced algorithms and technologies such as natural language processing and machine learning to analyze and interpret customer data more accurately. These systems can recognize nuanced patterns and contexts, leading to more reliable risk assessments and a reduction in false positives. For a typical financial institution monitoring KYC, typically 75%-85% of the alerts are false positives, with up to 25% reviewed by level-two senior analysts.[xix] These results into increased costs of compliance for most of the financial institutions.

POOR DATA QUALITY

False negatives in the context of KYC monitoring refer to situations where a client who is associated with a sanctioned entity or poses a high-risk profile is not identified for enhanced due diligence. This failure to detect and flag such clients can have serious consequences, including regulatory non-compliance, potential fines, enforcement actions, and reputational damage to the bank.

One of the key factors contributing to false negatives is poor data quality. Inaccurate data entry, incomplete information, outdated records, and human errors in data management can hinder the effectiveness of compliance screening processes. In India, there are many banks who have changed their core banking software multiple times. This change has led to deterioration in the quality of their data. Migration of data is never a perfect process and leads to leakages in the data.

When the data used for KYC screening is unreliable or inconsistent, there is a higher likelihood of missing important red flags and failing to identify clients who require closer scrutiny.

LACK OF DETAILED ALERTS

In the realm of KYC compliance, alerts are generated when there are specific activities or changes in corporate customer profiles that require closer scrutiny. However, one common challenge faced by compliance officers is that these alerts often lack sufficient detail, making it difficult for them to make informed and real-time risk-based decisions.

When alerts lack comprehensive information, compliance officers are forced to invest additional time and effort in investigating the underlying reasons behind the alert. For example, an alert might indicate a change in company directorships, but fail to provide details about the new directors involved. This lack of detail hampers the efficiency of compliance processes and can lead to delays in making well-informed decisions.

To overcome this challenge, it is essential for firms to work with a platform or technology solution that provides actionable information and detailed alerts. Such a platform should offer comprehensive data and contextual information about the specific activity triggering the alert. By receiving detailed alerts, compliance officers can quickly assess the situation, understand the nature of the change or activity, and make informed decisions based on the available information.

INADEQUATE RECORD KEEPING

Disparate systems refer to the situation where different data and information related to KYC activities are stored across various platforms or databases within an organization. This fragmentation can make it challenging to gather and consolidate all the necessary records when demonstrating compliance to regulators. It becomes difficult to provide a comprehensive and cohesive view of the activities performed and the decisions made during the KYC process.

Manual record-keeping, on the other hand, involves relying on paper-based documentation or relying on individual employees to maintain records in an ad-hoc manner. This approach increases the risk of errors, loss of information, and inconsistency in record-keeping practices. It can also make it challenging to retrieve and present the required information when faced with regulatory audits or inquiries.

To address these challenges, firms should consider implementing automated monitoring solutions. These solutions offer several advantages when it comes to record-keeping and compliance reporting. Firstly, automated monitoring solutions provide a centralized platform or system that consolidates all the relevant KYC records and activities. This allows for easy access to information and ensures that all relevant data is captured and stored in a structured and organized manner. Compliance officers and auditors can quickly retrieve the required information and gain a comprehensive view of the compliance efforts undertaken.

Secondly, automated solutions offer clear audit trails that document the activities performed throughout the KYC process. This includes details such as when alerts were generated, how they were investigated, and the actions taken in response. These audit trails serve as a transparent record of compliance activities, demonstrating adherence to regulatory requirements and providing evidence of due diligence.

Furthermore, automated monitoring solutions enable the recording of activities in a consistent and standardized manner. This reduces the risk of errors and omissions that can occur with manual record-keeping. The system can capture relevant data points automatically, ensuring accuracy and completeness of the records.

Finally, having an automated monitoring solution in place simplifies compliance reporting. With a centralized system and comprehensive records, firms can generate reports efficiently and accurately, showcasing their compliance efforts to regulators. This streamlines the reporting process and enhances the ability to meet regulatory expectations.

LIMITED CONFIGURABILITY

When it comes to ongoing monitoring in the KYC process, some solutions available in the market lack the necessary configurability to meet the specific needs of organizations. This can result in the generation of irrelevant alerts, which can be time-consuming and can divert resources away from more critical tasks. To address this challenge, it is crucial for organizations to work with a compliance partner that offers a highly configurable regulatory rules engine.

A highly configurable regulatory rules engine allows organizations to customize and adjust the rules that govern their ongoing monitoring processes. This means that they can tailor the system to align with their specific requirements and risk appetite. By having the ability to configure the rules, organizations can ensure that only relevant alerts are generated, reducing the noise and improving the efficiency of the monitoring process.

Furthermore, a configurable regulatory rules engine enables organizations to respond quickly to changing regulations. Regulatory requirements and risk landscapes are constantly evolving, and organizations need to adapt their monitoring practices accordingly. With a highly configurable system, organizations can easily modify the rules in real-time to comply with new regulations or changes in existing ones. This flexibility ensures that the monitoring process remains up-to-date and aligned with the regulatory environment.

Reducing irrelevant alerts has several benefits. First, it saves time and resources by allowing compliance teams to focus on alerts that are truly significant and require further investigation. This improves the overall efficiency of the compliance function and ensures that resources are allocated effectively.

Moreover, reducing irrelevant alerts helps prevent alert fatigue among compliance officers. When inundated with a large volume of irrelevant alerts, there is a risk of important alerts being overlooked or not given due attention. By minimizing irrelevant alerts, compliance officers can concentrate on the alerts that matter, enabling them to make informed decisions and take appropriate actions in a timely manner.

HOLISTIC APPROACH TO COMPLIANCE

As businesses face ever-increasing volumes of data, some have opted to rely solely on a "data provider" for their compliance solutions. However, many of these relationships involve adding data components to existing systems rather than adopting a holistic approach that comprehensively addresses compliance challenges and meets the necessary level of due diligence required by regulators.

A holistic approach to compliance should be adopted from the initial onboarding of customers throughout the entire customer lifecycle. This approach ensures that the business maintains a thorough understanding of its relationship with customers and meets regulatory requirements. While data-driven solutions incorporate data into the compliance process, they often fail to consider the bigger picture and the nuances that arise when transitioning from onboarding to ongoing monitoring.

By solely relying on a data-driven approach, organizations may experience limited configurability in terms of what triggers alerts, which can lead to wasted time and resources as inconsequential issues are needlessly flagged. Additionally, a data-driven approach may overlook important factors such as changes in legislation or the business's own risk appetite. These nuances require a comprehensive understanding of the business's unique context and objectives, which can only be achieved through a holistic approach to compliance.

Adopting a holistic approach allows organizations to align their compliance efforts with their overall business strategies and objectives. It ensures that compliance processes are integrated into the broader operational framework, taking into account factors such as evolving regulations, risk profiles, and the specific needs of the business and its customers. This comprehensive perspective enables organizations to effectively manage compliance throughout the customer lifecycle, from initial onboarding to ongoing monitoring and beyond.

AMBER MANAGEMENT MONITORING

Regulated businesses often encounter challenges when it comes to identifying and monitoring ambiguous results, commonly referred to as "ambers," within their compliance systems. These ambers represent cases or alerts that fall into a gray area, requiring further investigation or analysis to determine their significance and potential risks. Effectively managing these ambers is crucial to ensure compliance, allocate appropriate resources, and mitigate potential risks and penalties.

Recognizing and quantifying ambers can be a complex task. It involves identifying alerts or cases that do not fall clearly into the categories of true positives or false positives but require additional scrutiny. These ambiguous results can result from various factors such as incomplete information, conflicting data points, or unusual patterns that do not immediately indicate a violation or compliance issue.

Implementing an amber management approach is essential to address these challenges. This approach involves establishing a systematic process to identify, track, and report on ambers within the compliance systems. It provides a structured framework for managing these cases, enabling businesses to allocate appropriate resources, monitor progress, and make informed decisions regarding their significance.

By implementing effective amber management, businesses can gain better visibility into potential risks and compliance issues that may not be easily categorized. It allows for a focused and proactive approach to investigate and resolve these cases, minimizing the likelihood of regulatory penalties and reputational damage.

Having insight into ambers also enables businesses to identify any underlying trends or patterns that may require further analysis or adjustments to compliance processes. It provides valuable information for enhancing risk assessment strategies, improving data quality, and refining compliance protocols to address potential areas of vulnerability.

Furthermore, comprehensive reporting capabilities associated with amber management allow businesses to provide necessary evidence and documentation to regulators, demonstrating their proactive approach to compliance and risk management. This strengthens the organization's ability to meet regulatory requirements and fosters a culture of transparency and accountability.

ROLE OF FIU

The Financial Intelligence Unit-India (FIU-IND)[xx] is the central agency in India responsible for receiving, analyzing, and disseminating information related to suspicious financial transactions and activities. It is an independent body under the Ministry of Finance and operates as a national center for receiving, analyzing, and disseminating Suspicious Transaction Reports (STRs) and Cash Transaction Reports (CTRs) from reporting entities.

In the implementation of KYC guidelines in India, the FIU-IND plays a crucial role in ensuring compliance with anti-money laundering (AML) and counter-terrorist financing (CTF) measures. Here are the key roles and responsibilities of the FIU-IND:

- Receipt and Analysis of Reports: The FIU-IND receives STRs and CTRs from reporting entities, such as banks, financial institutions, and intermediaries. It analyzes the received information to identify suspicious transactions or activities that may be linked to money laundering, terrorist financing, or other illegal activities.

- Information Dissemination: Upon analysis, the FIU-IND disseminates the actionable intelligence to the relevant law enforcement agencies, such as the Central Bureau of Investigation (CBI), Enforcement Directorate (ED), or State Police Departments, for further investigation and enforcement action.
- Collaboration and Cooperation: The FIU-IND collaborates with domestic and international agencies involved in the fight against money laundering and terrorist financing. It exchanges information and cooperates with other FIUs globally to support investigations and enhance international cooperation in combating financial crimes.
- Policy Development and Guidance: The FIU-IND actively contributes to the development of policies, guidelines, and best practices related to AML and CTF measures. It provides guidance and support to reporting entities on complying with KYC regulations and reporting obligations.
- Monitoring and Compliance: The FIU-IND monitors the compliance of reporting entities with their reporting obligations and KYC guidelines. It conducts periodic inspections, audits, and assessments to ensure that reporting entities are adhering to the prescribed standards and procedures.

FIU-IND serves as a critical entity in the implementation of KYC guidelines in India by facilitating the reporting, analysis, and dissemination of suspicious transaction information. It acts as a bridge between reporting entities and law enforcement agencies, helping to combat financial crimes and protect the integrity of the financial system.

REGISTRATION WITH FIU-IND

It is necessary for every reporting entity to register itself on the FIU-Ind portal. In India, certain entities are required to register with the Financial Intelligence Unit-India (FIU-IND) and report suspicious transactions and cash transactions. The entities that are mandated to register with FIU-IND include:

- Banking Companies: This includes all commercial banks, cooperative banks, regional rural banks, and other banking institutions operating in India.
- Financial Institutions: Non-banking financial companies (NBFCs), housing finance companies (HFCs), payment system providers, and other financial institutions fall under this category.
- Intermediaries: Entities acting as intermediaries in securities markets, such as stockbrokers, depository participants, portfolio managers, investment advisors, and custodians, are required to register with FIU-IND.
- Money Changers: Authorized dealers in foreign exchange, commonly known as money changers, need to register with FIU-IND.
- Prepaid Payment Instrument Issuers: Entities issuing prepaid instruments such as prepaid cards, mobile wallets, and digital payment platforms are required to register with FIU-IND.
- Cooperative Societies: Cooperative credit societies, cooperative housing societies, and other cooperative societies involved in financial activities also fall under the purview of FIU-IND registration.

- Casinos: Casinos, both land-based and offshore, are required to register with FIU-IND due to the high-risk nature of their operations.

These entities are required to fulfill their reporting obligations to FIU-IND by submitting Suspicious Transaction Reports (STRs) and Cash Transaction Reports (CTRs) as per the prescribed formats and timelines. They must comply with the provisions of the Prevention of Money Laundering Act (PMLA) and related regulations issued by the Reserve Bank of India (RBI) and other regulatory authorities.

APPOINTMENT OF AML OFFICERS

Under the FIU-IND regime, it is a requirement for reporting entities to appoint an AML Officer, also referred to as the Principal Officer. The Principal Officer plays a crucial role in ensuring compliance with anti-money laundering (AML) and counter-terrorism financing (CTF) obligations. One of the key aspects of their role is to maintain effective communication with the Financial Intelligence Unit-India (FIU-IND).

PRINCIPAL OFFICER (PO)

The Principal Officer is a designated individual responsible for ensuring compliance with the obligations under the Prevention of Money Laundering Act (PMLA) and other related regulations. The key requirements for the appointment of a Principal Officer are as follows:

1. Every reporting entity, including banks, financial institutions, intermediaries, and other entities classified as reporting entities, must appoint a Principal Officer.

2. The Principal Officer should be an employee of the reporting entity and possess the necessary knowledge and expertise to fulfill the responsibilities associated with the role.
3. The appointment of the Principal Officer should be intimated to FIU-IND, and their details, such as name, designation, and contact information, should be provided.
4. The Principal Officer acts as the primary point of contact for all communications with FIU-IND, including reporting of suspicious transactions and other compliance-related matters.

Registration of Email ID with FIU-IND:

The reporting entity designates an AML Officer or Principal Officer who acts as a point of contact with FIU IND.

The AML Officer's email ID is registered with FIU-IND, ensuring direct communication and receipt of important notifications.

Receipt of Important Communications

- Circulars: FIU-IND issues circulars to provide updates on regulatory changes, clarifications, or new guidelines related to AML/CTF compliance. The AML Officer receives these circulars to stay informed about the latest developments.
- Guidance Notes: FIU-IND publishes guidance notes to assist reporting entities in understanding specific AML/CTF obligations, best practices, and procedures. The AML Officer receives these notes for

dissemination and implementation within the reporting entity.
- Research Papers: FIU-IND may release research papers or studies related to money laundering, terrorist financing, or emerging trends. These papers offer insights and analysis, which the AML Officer reviews to enhance their understanding and guide the reporting entity's compliance efforts.
- Red Flag Analyses: FIU-IND conducts red flag analyses to identify suspicious transaction patterns, activities, or indicators. The AML Officer receives these analyses to raise awareness within the reporting entity and strengthen the monitoring and reporting of potential suspicious transactions.

The AML Officer acts as a bridge between FIU-IND and the reporting entity, ensuring effective communication and the dissemination of crucial information. By receiving and reviewing circulars, guidance notes, research papers, and red flag analyses, the AML Officer stays updated on evolving AML/CTF requirements, regulatory expectations, and emerging risks. This information is then shared with relevant personnel within the reporting entity to promote compliance, enhance internal controls, and facilitate the reporting of suspicious transactions or activities to FIU-IND when necessary.

DESIGNATED DIRECTOR

The Designated Director is a key individual responsible for ensuring compliance with anti-money laundering (AML) and counter-terrorism financing (CTF) obligations within the reporting entity. The requirements related to the appointment of a Designated Director are as follows:

1. Every reporting entity, including entities classified as reporting entities under the PMLA, must appoint a Designated Director.
2. The Designated Director should be a director or partner of the reporting entity.
3. The Designated Director should possess the necessary knowledge and understanding of AML and CTF laws, regulations, and obligations.
4. The Designated Director is responsible for overseeing the implementation of AML/CTF policies and procedures, ensuring compliance with regulatory requirements, and acting as a point of contact for regulatory authorities.

These requirements are aimed at ensuring effective compliance with AML/CTF obligations and facilitating the smooth flow of information between reporting entities and FIU-IND.

While the Principal Officer focuses more on the operational aspects of AML/CTF compliance and acts as a communication link between the reporting entity and regulatory authorities, the Designated Director has a broader governance role, ensuring overall compliance and accountability within the reporting entity. Both roles are crucial in establishing a robust AML/CTF framework and maintaining a strong culture of compliance within the organization.

REPORTS TO BE SUBMITTED TO FIU

Reporting entities in India are required to submit various reports to the Financial Intelligence Unit India (FIU-IND) as part of their obligations under the anti-money laundering (AML) and counter-terrorism financing (CTF) framework. Here are some of the different types of reports that reporting entities may have to submit:

- Cash Transaction Report (CTR): Reporting entities, such as banks and financial institutions, are required to submit CTRs to the FIU-IND for cash transactions above a specified threshold. These reports capture details of large cash transactions, including the identity of the parties involved, the amount, and other relevant information.
- Suspicious Transaction Report (STR): Whenever a reporting entity detects a suspicious transaction or activity that may be indicative of money laundering or terrorist financing, they are obligated to file an STR with the FIU-IND. The STR provides details about the suspicious activity, such as the nature of the transaction, parties involved, and any other relevant information that may help in the investigation.[xxi]
- Counterfeit Currency Report (CCR): In cases where reporting entities come across counterfeit currency notes, they are required to file CCRs with the FIU-IND. These reports include information about the counterfeit notes, such as denomination, serial numbers, and any associated details that can assist in tracking the source or circulation of counterfeit currency.

- Non-Profit Organization Transaction Report (NTRO): Reporting entities that facilitate transactions for non-profit organizations (NPOs) need to submit NTROs to the FIU-IND. These reports capture information related to transactions carried out by NPOs, including the purpose of the transaction and any suspicious indicators, if observed.
- Cross-Border Wire Transfer Report (CBTR): Reporting entities involved in cross-border wire transfers are required to submit CBTRs to the FIU-IND. These reports contain details of the cross-border transactions, including the originator and beneficiary information, the amount transferred, and other relevant data.
- Terrorism Financing Intelligence Report (TFIR): In case reporting entities obtain any intelligence or information related to terrorism financing, they are obligated to submit TFIRs to the FIU-IND. These reports provide critical information that can aid in investigating and combating terrorism financing activities.

FUTURE OF KYC IN INDIA

Future of KYC in India will involve greater digitization, automation, and integration of advanced technologies to streamline processes, improve efficiency, and enhance the effectiveness of financial crime prevention measures

EMERGING TRENDS IN KYC

A robust KYC program comprises a Customer Identification Procedure (CIP) that involves collecting and validating customer data, which can be a challenging task. Counterfeit documents, obscured ownership structures, and complex transaction monitoring techniques like trade-based money laundering pose significant hurdles. To assist compliance and risk teams, financial institutions must embrace advanced technologies. Below, we explore three cutting-edge technology trends that are revolutionizing the process of gathering, verifying, screening, monitoring, and storing customer information.

DIGITIZATION AND AUTOMATION

the adoption of digital technologies is revolutionizing the way financial institutions handle KYC procedures. By embracing digitization and automation, these institutions can streamline the customer onboarding process, ensuring a smoother and more efficient experience for customers.

Through digitization, the cumbersome paper-based methods of collecting and verifying customer information are being replaced by digital platforms and tools. This transition allows financial institutions to expedite the KYC process, enabling customers to undergo verification more quickly and with less hassle. By digitizing the KYC process, institutions can also improve data accuracy, reducing the likelihood of errors that may arise from manual data entry or documentation.

Moreover, the integration of automation in KYC procedures brings about a host of benefits. By automating certain tasks and leveraging advanced technologies, financial institutions can enhance operational efficiency. Time-consuming and repetitive tasks can now be performed by automated systems, freeing up valuable resources and allowing staff to focus on more complex and critical aspects of the KYC process. This not only saves time and effort but also reduces the chances of human error, leading to more accurate and reliable KYC outcomes.

Additionally, the adoption of digital technologies and automation improves the overall management of customer information. Financial institutions can now effectively organize and verify the required data in a centralized digital repository, making it easier to access and analyze. This enhances the institutions' ability to monitor and maintain compliance with regulatory requirements.

Ultimately, the integration of digitization and automation in the KYC process brings benefits to both financial institutions and their customers. Customers can enjoy a faster and more streamlined onboarding experience, reducing the time and effort required to complete KYC procedures. Financial institutions, on the other hand, can operate more efficiently, ensuring compliance with regulatory standards while optimizing resource allocation.

RISK-BASED APPROACH

Indiaforensic, a renowned institution in the field of financial crime and compliance, provides a comprehensive certification program that focuses on the risk-based approach to AML (Anti-Money Laundering) and KYC (Know Your Customer). As regulators around the world, including those in India, recognize the importance of effectively combating financial crimes, they are encouraging financial institutions to adopt a risk-based approach to KYC procedures.

In a risk-based approach, the level of due diligence required for each customer is determined based on their individual risk profile. This means that customers are assessed and categorized according to their potential risk of involvement in money laundering, terrorist financing, or other illicit activities. By assigning different levels of scrutiny based on risk, financial institutions can allocate their resources more efficiently and focus their attention on higher-risk customers.

The risk-based approach to KYC offers several advantages. Firstly, it enables more targeted and tailored KYC processes. Instead of applying a one-size-fits-all approach, institutions can customize their due diligence efforts to match the risk associated with each customer. This allows for a more efficient allocation of resources, ensuring that the highest level of scrutiny is applied where it is most needed.

Furthermore, the risk-based approach promotes a more proactive and preventive approach to combating financial crimes. By identifying and assessing potential risks early on, institutions can implement appropriate controls and preventive measures to mitigate those risks. This not only strengthens their compliance efforts but also reduces the likelihood of being involved in illicit activities or inadvertently facilitating money laundering or terrorist financing.

In addition, the risk-based approach aligns with the principle of proportionality, where the level of due diligence is proportionate to the risk posed by the customer. This principle recognizes that not all customers pose the same level of risk and allows institutions to focus their resources on areas of higher concern. It also encourages a more efficient use of resources, as lower-risk customers can undergo a less burdensome KYC process, freeing up time and effort for more critical cases.

By offering a certification program on the risk-based approach to AML and KYC, Indiaforensic equips professionals with the necessary knowledge and skills to implement this approach effectively. Participants in the program gain a deep understanding of risk assessment methodologies, risk profiling techniques, and the application of risk-based due diligence. This empowers them to contribute to more targeted and efficient KYC processes within their organizations, ultimately enhancing overall compliance efforts and risk management capabilities.

USE OF ARTIFICIAL INTELLIGENCE (AI) AND MACHINE LEARNING (ML)

AI and ML technologies are being leveraged to analyze large volumes of customer data, identify suspicious patterns or behaviours, and enhance fraud detection capabilities.

Artificial Intelligence (AI) is transforming the landscape of Know Your Customer (KYC) and Anti-Money Laundering (AML) compliance. It encompasses a range of related technologies that have the power to automate workflows and analyze large volumes of diverse data quickly. By harnessing AI in KYC/AML processes, several significant benefits emerge:

Link Analysis

AI-driven link analysis techniques enable investigators to navigate complex networks of relationships and transactions. This aids in uncovering hidden connections and drawing insightful conclusions that may not be evident from individual pieces of information. Link analysis also enhances automated decision-making by integrating structured data with linkage data represented as a graph, identifying dubious jurisdictions, companies, and ultimate beneficial owners (UBOs).

"AI-powered solutions not only automate operational tasks but also provide advanced capabilities for analyzing structured and unstructured data, resulting in superior insights."

Pattern Recognition

Money launderers often employ sophisticated techniques to conceal illicit funds, making it challenging to detect their activities. Leading banks worldwide are transitioning from rule-based systems to AI-based solutions that exhibit greater resilience and intelligence in identifying anti-money laundering patterns. FICO, for instance, has developed Anti-Financial Crime Solutions utilizing unsupervised Bayesian learning techniques. [xxii] These models leverage customer behavior analysis to drive investigations and potentially trigger Suspicious Activity Reports (SARs).

Unstructured Data Analysis

AI in KYC leverages Natural Language Processing (NLP) and supervised machine learning to analyze unstructured content, such as adverse media. NLP-based AI can extract metadata, identify entities, and understand the context and purpose of specific document sections. This enables more effective analysis and risk assessment, complementing structured data analysis.

BIOMETRIC AUTHENTICATION

Biometric technologies, such as fingerprint or facial recognition, are increasingly being used for identity verification during the KYC process. These technologies provide a higher level of security and reduce the risk of identity fraud.

Social Biometrics

Social biometrics is an emerging trend in the field of KYC (Know Your Customer) and AML (Anti-Money Laundering). It involves leveraging a person's digital footprint from social media platforms like Google, Facebook, Twitter, and others to gather valuable information about an individual that may not be available through traditional sources. By analyzing social biometrics data, financial institutions can obtain insights into customers, including millennials, the underbanked, and the unbanked, who may have limited credit history but maintain a significant social presence.

One of the advantages of social biometrics is its ability to provide a dynamic and constantly evolving view of an individual's exposure. As the information is derived from online platforms, it reflects real-time activities and updates. When combined with traditional credit and KYC data, social biometrics enhances risk assessment capabilities, particularly in identifying identity theft and fraud.

The integration of social biometrics into KYC/AML processes offers several benefits for financial institutions. Firstly, it provides a more comprehensive and holistic understanding of customer profiles, enabling a more accurate assessment of risk. This, in turn, improves the effectiveness of KYC and AML measures. Secondly, leveraging social biometrics can lead to significant cost savings for financial institutions by streamlining and automating certain aspects of the KYC process. Lastly, it enhances the customer experience by expediting the onboarding process and reducing the need for extensive documentation, benefiting both the customers and the financial institutions.

Blockchain Technology

Blockchain technology has the potential to significantly enhance Know Your Customer (KYC) processes by addressing various pain points associated with traditional methods. However, several challenges must be overcome for widespread adoption and integration of blockchain into existing systems and regulations.

Scalability is a critical challenge that needs to be addressed. Blockchain networks, especially public ones like Bitcoin and Ethereum, have limitations in terms of transaction processing speed and capacity. As KYC processes involve a large volume of customer data and transactions, blockchain solutions need to demonstrate scalability to handle the growing demands of the industry.

Interoperability is another challenge to consider. KYC processes involve multiple entities such as banks, regulatory bodies, and other financial institutions. For blockchain to be effective, it needs to seamlessly integrate and interact with existing systems and databases. Achieving interoperability between different blockchain platforms and legacy systems is crucial for the widespread adoption of blockchain-based KYC solutions.

Regulatory compliance is a critical aspect of KYC processes. Existing regulations and compliance requirements may need to be revised or adapted to accommodate blockchain technology. Regulatory bodies need to establish guidelines and frameworks that ensure the legality, security, and privacy of customer data on blockchain platforms. Additionally, compliance with data protection regulations and privacy laws, such as GDPR, must be ensured when implementing blockchain-based KYC solutions.

Furthermore, the cost and complexity of implementing blockchain technology can be significant barriers to adoption. Organizations need to invest in the development, implementation, and maintenance of blockchain infrastructure. They also need to train staff and stakeholders on blockchain technology and its implications for KYC processes. Overcoming these barriers requires a strong business case, collaboration among industry participants, and support from regulatory authorities.

Despite these challenges, the potential benefits of blockchain in KYC are substantial. Blockchain can provide a secure, transparent, and immutable platform for storing and sharing customer data. It can enable efficient and trusted verification processes, reduce duplication of efforts, and enhance data accuracy. Blockchain's decentralized nature ensures data security and protects against unauthorized access and tampering. It also empowers customers by allowing them to control their personal data and consent to its use.

POTENTIAL IMPACT OF EMERGING TECHNOLOGIES ON KYC

Improved Efficiency: Emerging technologies can automate manual processes, reduce paperwork, and expedite the KYC process, leading to faster customer onboarding and reduced operational costs.

Enhanced Security: Technologies like biometrics and blockchain offer increased security and accuracy in identity verification, reducing the risk of identity theft and fraud.

Better Customer Experience: Digital KYC solutions provide a seamless and convenient onboarding experience for customers, eliminating the need for physical document submission and in-person verification.

Advanced Risk Assessment: AI and ML algorithms can analyze vast amounts of customer data and detect patterns that human analysts might miss, leading to more effective risk assessment and fraud prevention.

Cross-Institutional Collaboration: Blockchain-based KYC solutions can enable secure sharing of customer information among financial institutions, improving customer convenience and reducing duplication of efforts.

FUTURE OF KYC REGULATIONS IN INDIA

The future of Know Your Customer (KYC) regulations in India is likely to involve further advancements and reforms to enhance customer due diligence, strengthen anti-money laundering (AML) measures, and promote a more robust financial ecosystem.

It's important to note that the future of KYC regulations in India is subject to evolving regulatory landscape, technological advancements, and changing market dynamics. The specific reforms and developments may vary over time based on the priorities and initiatives undertaken by regulatory authorities, government agencies, and industry stakeholders.

Here are some key aspects that may shape the future of KYC regulations in India:

UNIFIED KYC

The Unified KYC framework is an initiative led by the Reserve Bank of India (RBI) to establish a centralized repository of KYC (Know Your Customer) records that can be accessed by banks and financial institutions. The goal of this framework is to streamline the KYC process, eliminate duplication of efforts, enhance data sharing, and improve the overall customer experience.

Under the current system, when an individual opens an account or avails services from multiple banks or financial institutions, they are required to undergo the KYC process separately for each institution. This leads to redundant paperwork, repeated verification of identity and address proofs, and delays in the onboarding process.

The Unified KYC framework aims to address these challenges by creating a centralized database where customer KYC records can be stored securely. This database will contain verified customer information, such as identity proofs, address proofs, and other relevant documents, which have been authenticated by the participating institutions.

With the implementation of the Unified KYC framework, when a customer approaches a new bank or financial institution for services, the institution can access the customer's KYC information from the central repository with the customer's consent. This eliminates the need for the customer to undergo the KYC process again and reduces the paperwork and time involved.

The centralized repository ensures that KYC records are standardized, consistent, and readily available to authorized entities. It also enables effective data sharing among institutions while maintaining data privacy and security. By eliminating duplication of KYC efforts, the framework promotes efficiency, cost savings, and a seamless onboarding experience for customers.

The Unified KYC framework enhances compliance with regulatory requirements by enabling better monitoring and supervision of customer data. It helps financial institutions in performing due diligence and risk assessment more effectively, as they have access to comprehensive and verified customer information.

DIGITAL TRANSFORMATION

The future of KYC in India will be increasingly digital, with greater reliance on technology-enabled solutions for customer identification, verification, and ongoing monitoring.

ENHANCED DATA SECURITY

Data protection laws and regulations play a critical role in ensuring that individuals' personal information is handled securely and used appropriately. Compliance with these laws, such as the General Data Protection Regulation (GDPR) in Europe or the Personal Data Protection Bill in India, will continue to be a significant aspect of KYC regulations.

Financial institutions and service providers will need to implement robust data protection measures to ensure that customer information is handled securely throughout the KYC process. This includes secure storage and transmission of data, encryption techniques, access controls, and regular audits to identify and address any vulnerabilities.

An important consideration in the future of KYC regulations is the need to obtain customer consent for collecting, storing, and processing their personal data. Clear and transparent information about how customer data will be used and shared is essential to build trust and comply with privacy requirements.

Regulatory authorities will likely introduce guidelines and standards for data protection in the context of KYC processes.

Financial institutions will be expected to implement measures to protect customer data from unauthorized access, misuse, or data breaches. This may involve implementing strong authentication methods, robust data encryption, and regular monitoring of data access and usage.

As technology evolves, innovative solutions such as decentralized identity systems, secure multi-party computation, or homomorphic encryption may emerge to enhance data protection in KYC processes. These technologies aim to provide privacy-enhancing features while still enabling effective identity verification and risk assessment.

Collaborative Efforts: Regulatory bodies, financial institutions, and technology providers will collaborate to develop standardized KYC frameworks, promote interoperability, and facilitate data sharing while ensuring data privacy and security.

PRACTICE QUESTIONS

What is the purpose of the Prevention of Money Laundering Act (PMLA) in India?
a) Regulating financial institutions
b) Facilitating cross-border transactions
c) Combating money laundering
d) Promoting financial inclusion
Correct answer: c) Combating money laundering

Which regulatory body sets international standards for combating money laundering and terrorist financing?
a) RBI
b) FATF
c) UIDAI
d) PMLA
Correct answer: b) FATF

In which year was the Aadhaar-based e-KYC system introduced in India?
a) 2004
b) 2012
c) 2016
d) 2021
Correct answer: c) 2016

What is one benefit of KYC compliance in India?
a) Preventing financial crimes
b) Reducing infrastructure challenges
c) Increasing fraudulent practices
d) Limiting customer trust
Correct answer: a) Preventing financial crimes

Which entities are responsible for implementing KYC procedures in India?
a) Government agencies
b) Non-profit organizations
c) Banks and financial institutions
d) Educational institutions
Correct answer: c) Banks and financial institutions

What are the challenges in implementing KYC in India?
a) Limited access to identification documents
b) High awareness of KYC norms
c) Abundance of infrastructure
d) Frequent fraudulent practices
Correct answer: a) Limited access to identification documents

What role do banks play in KYC procedures?
a) Monitoring transactions for suspicious activities
b) Promoting customer awareness of KYC norms
c) Providing identification documents to customers
d) Implementing KYC regulations for the government

PRACTICE QUESTIONS

Correct answer: a) Monitoring transactions for suspicious activities

What is the primary purpose of KYC regulations in India?
a) Ensuring compliance with international regulations
b) Streamlining cross-border transactions
c) Mitigating the risk of financial crimes
d) Expanding financial services to underbanked populations
Correct answer: c) Mitigating the risk of financial crimes

What is Aadhaar-based eKYC?
a) A manual verification process conducted at the bank
b) A method of verifying identity remotely using Aadhaar data
c) A physical visit to the KYC Registration Agency
d) A verification process using only biometric information
Correct answer: b) A method of verifying identity remotely using Aadhaar data

What information is required for Aadhaar OTP-based verification?
a) Aadhaar number and mobile number
b) Aadhaar number and email address
c) Aadhaar number and physical address
d) Aadhaar number and PAN number
Correct answer: a) Aadhaar number and mobile number

What is the purpose of biometric-based verification in Aadhaar eKYC?
a) To collect personal information for marketing purposes
b) To match biometric data with the Aadhaar database
c) To generate a unique identification number for customers
d) To provide customers with a physical Aadhaar card
Correct answer: b) To match biometric data with the Aadhaar database

How does Aadhaar-based eKYC benefit customers?
a) It requires physical visits to the bank for verification
b) It increases the cost and time involved in the KYC process
c) It allows customers to verify their identity remotely
d) It eliminates the need for a mobile number for verification
Correct answer: c) It allows customers to verify their identity remotely

What is DigiLocker?
a) An online storage service for Aadhaar cards
b) A government agency that issues Aadhaar numbers
c) A biometric scanner used for Aadhaar verification
d) A mobile application for Aadhaar-based eKYC
Correct answer: a) An online storage service for Aadhaar cards

What is the Puttaswamy Aadhaar test?
a) A verification process using Aadhaar OTP
b) A Supreme Court judgment on Aadhaar's constitutionality
c) A method of biometric verification in Aadhaar eKYC
d) A government initiative for financial inclusion
Correct answer: b) A Supreme Court judgment on Aadhaar's constitutionality

What concerns have been raised regarding Aadhaar-based KYC?
a) Privacy and security issues

PRACTICE QUESTIONS

b) Lack of government support
c) Inconvenience for customers
d) Limited availability of Aadhaar cards
Correct answer: a) Privacy and security issues

What did the Supreme Court of India establish in the Puttaswamy Aadhaar test?
a) The mandatory use of Aadhaar for all services
b) The right to privacy as a fundamental right
c) The exclusion of biometric data from Aadhaar
d) The requirement of physical verification for KYC
Correct answer: b) The right to privacy as a fundamental right

What is the purpose of KYC in casinos?
a) To track customer spending habits
b) To prevent money laundering and terrorist financing
c) To provide personalized customer service
d) To verify the legal gambling age
Correct answer: b) To prevent money laundering and terrorist financing

Question: In the real estate sector, what is the primary objective of KYC?
a) To verify the buyer's credit history
b) To ensure the property is legally owned
c) To assess the buyer's financial capability
d) To identify and prevent fraudulent transactions
Correct answer: d) To identify and prevent fraudulent transactions

Question: What is the role of KYC in the telecom industry?
a) To verify the customer's identity for SIM card activation
b) To monitor internet usage patterns
c) To determine the customer's creditworthiness
d) To provide targeted advertisements to customers
Correct answer: a) To verify the customer's identity for SIM card activation

Question: In the banking sector, what is the purpose of KYC?
a) To track customers' daily transactions
b) To identify potential money laundering activities
c) To provide investment advice to customers
d) To issue credit cards to eligible customers
Correct answer: b) To identify potential money laundering activities

Question: Which of the following documents is commonly used for KYC in the casino industry?
a) Passport
b) Utility bill
c) Driving license
d) Social security card
Correct answer: a) Passport

Question: What does KYC stand for in the real estate sector?
a) Know Your Contract
b) Keep Your Credentials

PRACTICE QUESTIONS

c) Know Your Customer
d) Keep Your Certificates
Correct answer: c) Know Your Customer

Question: In the telecom industry, why is KYC necessary for SIM card activation?
a) To determine the customer's preferred mobile plan
b) To authenticate the customer's phone model
c) To ensure compliance with regulatory requirements
d) To offer discounts on data packages
Correct answer: c) To ensure compliance with regulatory requirements

Question: Which regulatory authority oversees KYC in the banking sector?
a) Securities and Exchange Board of India (SEBI)
b) Telecom Regulatory Authority of India (TRAI)
c) Reserve Bank of India (RBI)
d) Real Estate Regulatory Authority (RERA)
Correct answer: c) Reserve Bank of India (RBI)

Question: What is the main objective of KYC in the real estate sector?
a) To verify the seller's source of funds
b) To assess the property's market value
c) To analyze the buyer's credit score
d) To prevent money laundering and fraud
Correct answer: d) To prevent money laundering and fraud

Question: How does KYC help casinos in preventing illegal activities?
a) By monitoring players' gambling behavior
b) By verifying the source of funds for high rollers
c) By conducting background checks on casino employees
d) By enforcing age restrictions for entry
Correct answer: b) By verifying the source of funds for high rollers

Which of the following is a key provision of RBI Master Directions on KYC?
a) Customer Acceptance Policy
b) Transaction Monitoring Policy
c) Employee Training Policy
d) Marketing and Sales Policy
Correct answer: a) Customer Acceptance Policy

How should customers be categorized under the KYC framework?
a) High, medium, and low-risk categories
b) Red, yellow, and green-risk categories
c) Tier 1, tier 2, and tier 3-risk categories
d) A, B, C-risk categories
Correct answer: a) High, medium, and low-risk categories

What does CDD stand for in the context of KYC?
a) Customer Due Diligence
b) Cash Deposit Documentation
c) Credit Decision Determination
d) Compliance and Documentation Duties

PRACTICE QUESTIONS

Correct answer: a) Customer Due Diligence

Under the simplified KYC process, which documents can banks rely on for low-risk customers?
a) Passport and Driving License
b) Aadhaar, PAN Card, or other reliable documents
c) Utility bills and Rental Agreement
d) Employment ID and School ID
Correct answer: b) Aadhaar, PAN Card, or other reliable documents

What does EDD stand for in the context of KYC?
a) Enhanced Documentation and Disclosure
b) Extended Due Diligence
c) Excessive Documentation and Data
d) Enhanced Due Diligence
Correct answer: d) Enhanced Due Diligence

What is the responsibility of banks regarding the reporting of suspicious transactions?
a) Report to the Reserve Bank of India
b) Report to the Ministry of Finance
c) Report to the Financial Intelligence Unit-India (FIU-IND)
d) Report to the Indian Banks' Association (IBA)
Correct answer: c) Report to the Financial Intelligence Unit-India (FIU-IND)

Which entity is responsible for overseeing KYC compliance in India?
a) Indian Banks' Association (IBA)
b) Reserve Bank of India (RBI)
c) Securities and Exchange Board of India (SEBI)
d) Financial Intelligence Unit-India (FIU-IND)
Correct answer: b) Reserve Bank of India (RBI)

Can banks outsource KYC-related activities to third-party service providers?
a) Yes, without any oversight required
b) Yes, but with full exemption from compliance
c) No, outsourcing is not allowed for KYC activities
d) Yes, but with adequate oversight and responsibility
Correct answer: d) Yes, but with adequate oversight and responsibility

What should banks consider while conducting KYC for cross-border transactions?
a) Only follow the KYC requirements of the home country
b) Only follow the KYC requirements of the host country
c) Follow the due diligence requirements of both the home and host countries
d) No KYC requirements are applicable for cross-border transactions
Correct answer: c) Follow the due diligence requirements of both the home and host countries

What is one of the main benefits of implementing a robust KYC process?
a) Enhanced customer experience
b) Higher profitability for the institution
c) Reduced operational costs

d) Increased market share
Correct answer: c) Reduced operational costs

What is a potential challenge in implementing KYC procedures?
a) Slower customer onboarding process
b) Limited customer data for analysis
c) Insufficient regulatory oversight
d) Inadequate employee training
Correct answer: a) Slower customer onboarding process

How does KYC help in preventing fraud and financial crimes?
a) By verifying the source of funds
b) By providing insurance against losses
c) By ensuring high returns on investments
d) By offering attractive interest rates
Correct answer: a) By verifying the source of funds

What is one of the advantages of using technology in KYC processes?
a) Increased manual errors
b) Limited scalability
c) Improved accuracy and efficiency
d) Reduced customer trust
Correct answer: c) Improved accuracy and efficiency

What is a challenge associated with KYC data management?
a) Inadequate data storage capacity
b) Limited availability of customer data
c) Difficulty in data retrieval
d) Inability to comply with data protection laws
Correct answer: a) Inadequate data storage capacity

How does KYC contribute to regulatory compliance?
a) By increasing bureaucratic procedures
b) By facilitating money laundering activities
c) By ensuring adherence to anti-money laundering laws
d) By promoting unethical business practices
Correct answer: c) By ensuring adherence to anti-money laundering laws

What is one of the benefits of KYC for financial institutions?
a) Increased risk of reputational damage
b) Improved customer trust and loyalty
c) Higher chances of data breaches
d) Decreased compliance with regulations
Correct answer: b) Improved customer trust and loyalty

What is a potential challenge in maintaining up-to-date KYC records?
a) Limited access to customer information
b) Inadequate staff training
c) Inconsistent regulatory guidelines
d) Frequent changes in customer contact details
Correct answer: d) Frequent changes in customer contact details

How does KYC help in detecting and preventing identity theft?

PRACTICE QUESTIONS

a) By sharing customer data with unauthorized entities
b) By reducing customer privacy and confidentiality
c) By verifying the authenticity of customer identities
d) By increasing the risk of data breaches
Correct answer: c) By verifying the authenticity of customer identities

What is one of the benefits of a well-implemented KYC process for society?
a) Increased financial exclusion
b) Limited access to financial services
c) Reduced instances of money laundering and terrorist financing
d) Higher risk of fraud in the financial system
Correct answer: c) Reduced instances of money laundering and terrorist financing

What is the primary role of FIU-IND in combating money laundering?
a) Prosecuting money launderers
b) Investigating financial crimes
c) Collecting and analyzing financial intelligence
d) Implementing regulatory policies
Correct answer: c) Collecting and analyzing financial intelligence

Which organization is responsible for operating FIU-IND in India?
a) Reserve Bank of India (RBI)
b) Securities and Exchange Board of India (SEBI)
c) Ministry of Finance
d) Central Bureau of Investigation (CBI)
Correct answer: c) Ministry of Finance

What does FIU-IND do with the financial intelligence it collects?
a) Shares it with foreign intelligence agencies
b) Publishes it for public awareness
c) Uses it to issue penalties to financial institutions
d) Shares it with law enforcement agencies for investigations
Correct answer: d) Shares it with law enforcement agencies for investigations

Which of the following activities is considered a red flag for potential money laundering?
a) Frequent international wire transfers
b) Regular salary deposits
c) Small cash withdrawals
d) Routine credit card payments
Correct answer: a) Frequent international wire transfers

How does FIU-IND contribute to the prevention and detection of money laundering?
a) By conducting audits of financial institutions
b) By providing training programs to bank employees
c) By implementing stringent AML/CFT regulations
d) By analyzing suspicious transaction reports (STRs)
Correct answer: d) By analyzing suspicious transaction reports (STRs)

PRACTICE QUESTIONS

What is the purpose of filing a suspicious transaction report (STR) with FIU-IND?
a) To initiate criminal proceedings against the involved parties
b) To alert FIU-IND about potential money laundering activities
c) To request a detailed investigation by FIU-IND
d) To seek guidance on compliance with AML/CFT regulations
Correct answer: b) To alert FIU-IND about potential money laundering activities

How does FIU-IND collaborate with other countries in combating money laundering?
a) By sharing financial intelligence with foreign counterparts
b) By conducting joint investigations with foreign agencies
c) By imposing economic sanctions on non-compliant nations
d) By providing financial assistance to developing countries
Correct answer: a) By sharing financial intelligence with foreign counterparts

Which law empowers FIU-IND to receive, analyze, and disseminate financial intelligence in India?
a) Prevention of Money Laundering Act (PMLA)
b) Foreign Exchange Management Act (FEMA)
c) Income Tax Act
d) Indian Penal Code (IPC)
Correct answer: a) Prevention of Money Laundering Act (PMLA)

What measures does FIU-IND undertake to ensure the confidentiality of financial intelligence?
a) Publishing reports in the public domain
b) Sharing information through social media channels
c) Implementing secure data storage and access protocols
d) Disclosing sensitive information to the media
Correct answer: c) Implementing secure data storage and access protocols

REFERENCES

[i] Financial Action Task Force. (2012). International Standards on Combating Money Laundering and the Financing of Terrorism & Proliferation. https://www.fatf-gafi.org/media/fatf/documents/recommendations/pdfs/FATF_Recommendations.pdf

[ii] Reserve Bank of India. (2021). Know Your Customer (KYC) guidelines - Anti-Money Laundering Standards. https://www.rbi.org.in/scripts/NotificationUser.aspx?Id=12981&Mode=0

[iii] https://egazette.nic.in/WriteReadData/2023/245764.pdf

[iv] Digilocker Government Portal https://www.digilocker.gov.in/

[v] Central KYC Registry https://www.ckycindia.in/ckyc/index.php

[vi] https://www.india.com/business/rbi-slaps-rs-3-06-crore-fine-on-amazon-pay-india-over-non-compliance-with-kyc-norms-5926006/

[vii] https://www.thequint.com/news/india/china-monitoring-indian-personalitites-zhenhua-data-scraping

[viii] RBI Master Directions on KYC https://www.rbi.org.in/Scripts/BS_ViewMasDirections.aspx?id=11566#9

[ix] Voters Database https://www.nvsp.in/

[x] Judicial Data Grid https://njdg.ecourts.gov.in/njdgnew/index.php

[xi] Digital Land Records https://dilrmp.gov.in/#

[xii] Central Fingerprint Bureau https://ncrb.gov.in/en/finger-print-india

[xiii] Central Vehicle Registry https://vahan.parivahan.gov.in/paidnrservices/

[xiv] National Skills Registry https://nationalskillsregistry.com/aboutus.htm

[xv] Disability Card https://www.swavlambancard.gov.in/

[xvi] CERSAI https://www.cersai.org.in/CERSAI/home.prg

[xvii] CPGRAMS https://pgportal.gov.in/

[xviii] National Knowledge Network https://nkn.gov.in/en/

[xix] https://www.theglobaltreasurer.com/2015/10/08/false-positives-a-growing-headache/

[xx] FIU India Website https://fiuindia.gov.in/

[xxi] Obligations of NBFCs to File STR and CTR https://www.rbi.org.in/commonman/English/Scripts/Notification.aspx?Id=530

[xxii] https://www.fico.com/blogs/unsupervised-learning-part-2-aml-connection

Printed in Poland
by Amazon Fulfillment
Poland Sp. z o.o., Wrocław